D1429310

ROWDY RHYMES AND
REC-IM-ITATIONS

ROWDY RHYMES AND REC-IM-ITATIONS

VINCENT CAPRANI

Gill & Macmillan

Gill & Macmillan
Hume Avenue, Park West, Dublin 12
with associated companies throughout the world
www.gillmacmillan.ie

978 07171 5019 9

Design and print origination by Carole Lynch
Illustrations by Derry Dillon
Printed and bound by ScandBook AB, Sweden

This book is typeset in Linotype Minion and
Neue Helvetica.

The paper used in this book comes from the wood pulp of
managed forests. For every tree felled, at least one tree is
planted, thereby renewing natural resources.

A CIP catalogue record for this book is available
from the British Library.

5 4 3 2 1

CONTENTS

BEGINNINGS

I was born in a wilderness
In a jungle of brick and stone
In a dank and grimy canyon
Where each man stood alone.
I was reared in a fetid alley
In a criss-cross maze of lanes
Flanked by the toilers' hovels
Which were coloured by misery stains;
Where the rain was icy needles
And the sun was a truant light
And the winter wind was knife-like
And the snow was never white
But slushed from the age-old shuffle
Of the time-battered boots of the poor,
Where most of the folk went hungry
And death was swift and sure.

But once in a while came a balladeer
Or a blink-a-blonk banjo man
Or a fiddlin' fool with a resined bow
Begging pennies for his can;
Or a winsome lass with a carefree song
And a voice like rippling gold
Each note like a jewelled finger
That flicked away the cold
Though some of their tunes held sadness
And the echo of ancient wrongs
I could glimpse a kind of glory
In every one of their songs,

And when they sang of youthful love
My heart soared to the sky
And the damp grey walls of our alley
Never seemed half so high,
And the rain was a gentle moisture
And the wind was not so cold
And the sun would open its purse-strings
And squander its coins of gold.

ROWDY RHYMES AND LIFFEYSIDE LAMPOONS

"Let me make the ballads, and who will make the laws," wrote Andrew Fletcher in 1703. Even before that date — and ever since with a mischievous disregard for both the laws of libel and the canons of poetry — Dubliners have been making ballads, 'rec-im-itations' and parodies, commenting in verse form on everything from social events, public affairs, the city's monuments and institutions, politics, murder cases, sporting events, their fellow citizens and street 'characters', etc.

There was little that was news-worthy, topical — or sometimes even scurrilous and bawdy! — that escaped either the pens or the rough-and-ready 'pomes' of the early ballad-makers. For more than 200 years, right up until the twenties and thirties of the last century, the popular tunes and lampoons were sold on the streets of Dublin. "Latest songs, penny each!" … broadsheets of ballads and doggerel, crudely printed on single sheets of cheap paper, were hawked about by ragamuffin vendors, who, as often as not, recited a stanza or two of the current 'hit' as an enticement to the purchaser.

Thomas Street was the best pitch in the old days. With its open-air market and fair combined (especially on such occasions as Christmas Eve, when last-minute purchases could be made from street stalls or horse-drawn carts pulled up by the footpath) the raucous voices of the balladeers and verse vendors soared above the noise and bustle. There were ballads to commemorate patriotic subjects, Parnell of Avondale, Home Rule, The Howth Gun-Running; chuckle-raising 'epics' of canal barges and inland 'voyages' like The Cruise of the Calabar, The Thirteenth Lock, The Wreck of the Vartry; and even tributes to Dublin street traders like Mickey Baggs, The Twangman and Biddy Mulligan the Pride of the Coombe. Likewise the various fish, vegetable and cattle markets — all with their adjacent pubs — were places to go for the latest rhyming commentaries or 'stop press' ballads on which the printer's ink was still wet.

The printer, it should be added, was not infrequently held responsible for the eccentric and mischievous outpourings of the anonymous scribe. Arigho (who, in the early years of that century printed the still popular ballad which dealt with a 'hooley' of ragmen in Ash Street) was for a long time after persecuted by the various 'notabilities' mentioned in The Ragman's Ball. Humpy Soodelum, Billy Boland, Grace and Dunlavin all demanded 'largesse' for the unauthorised use of their names, exacting their own justice under the law of libel by demanding to be treated to free drink whenever they happened on poor Mr Arigho!

But many of the ballads, in addition to showing the Dubliner's instinct for the value of words and wit, also provide a handy and easily accessible guide to the ordinary occurrences of life and a glimpse into remote traditions. The following verses (which first appeared about 1910) are almost a directory of Dublin trades at the time and of the streets wherein they were plied, and as such they tell us something of our social history:

> *On George's Quay I first began*
> *And there became a porter;*
> *Me and my master soon fell out*
> *Which cut my acquaintance shorter.*
> *In Sackville street a pastry cook,*
> *In James's street a baker,*
> *In Cork street I did coffins make*
> *In Eustace street a preacher …*

The lengthy saga goes on to list the streets of grocers, grinders, clothes dryers, shoe sellers, hatters, sawyers, lawyers, brokers, drovers, glovers, booksellers, carpenters, butchers, tailors, drapers, 'bacco pipe makers, gilders, coach-makers etc.; and ends with …

In High street I sold hosiery,
In Patrick street I sold all blades;
So if you wish to know my name
They call me Jack of All Trades.

But who was 'Jack of All Trades'? And who were the other nameless rhymesters who enriched the lore and the traditions of our city? Perhaps we'll never know. But one thing is almost certain — Dubliners will still be singing their merry street ballads a hundred years from now.

The University men frequently penned ballads and doggerel. Goldsmith composed and sold such ballads on the streets and then quietly mingled with the motley crowd to watch the effect of his rhyming words on the audience. Charles Lever was not only a keen student of ballad literature but, in his Trinity days, went about the most frequented parts of the city in a hired uniform singing his own compositions. In the true style of the regular or 'professional' ballad-makers he showed scant respect for the susceptibilities of 'his betters':

O, Dublin City, there is no doubting
Bates every city upon the say:
'Tis there you'd hear O'Connell spouting,
And see Lady Morgan making tay.
For 'tis the capital of the finest nation
With charming peasantry on a fruitful sod,
Fighting like divils for conciliation
And hating each other for the love of God.

Trinity's Edwin Hamilton MA, whose book entitled *Dublin Doggerels* was published by Smith of Dame Street in 1877, and later reprinted in London, made mild fun of many Dublin institutions such as his alma mater, the GPO, Zoological Gardens, St Stephen's Green, the Four Courts and the River Liffey:

> *In the West the Liffey rises,*
> *In the East its course is done:*
> *Thus the River L despises*
> *The example of the sun.*

The patriot and statesman Arthur Griffith is credited with the authorship of the Grand Canal 'epic', 'The Thirteenth Lock', and his contemporaries, James Joyce and Oliver St John Gogarty, also, from time to time, indulged in the lampooning verse. Indeed, Joyce's final and curious novel takes its title from a popular Dublin ballad of more than a century ago:

Whack fol the da, dance to your partner,
Welt the flure, your trotters shake,
Wasn't it the truth I told you,
Lots of fun at Finnegan's Wake.

And his fictional character 'plump Buck Mulligan' — in real life the poet, wit, surgeon Dr Oliver St John Gogarty — penned the following lines:

I will live in Ringsend,
With a red-headed whore,
And the fan-light gone in
Where it lights the halldoor;
And listen each night
For her querulous shout,
As at last she streels in
And the pubs empty out.

Perhaps the most prolific of the Dublin ballad-makers was Michael Moran of Faddle Alley in the Liberties. Born in the 1790s, and blind almost from birth, he was sent out by his penurious parents to beg — and then later to rhyme and recite — at the street corners and the bridges over the Liffey. Moran had a prodigious memory and a vast repertoire of romantic, religious, rowdy and rollicking chants which he could call upon at will. From the best known of his religious recitations, 'St Mary of Egypt' — which tells of an Egyptian harlot who is converted to righteousness by Bishop Zozimus — Moran earned the nickname by which he was after remembered, 'Zozimus'. To him are attributed many of the nineteenth-century street ballads, including the still popular 'In Agypt's Land', wherein — and with the nasally twang of the true

Liffeysider — he parodies the intolerable solemnity of the religious verse of the previous century.

When Zozimus died in April 1846, all the city's ballad singers with fiddles and the like came to his wake in the narrow, dingy room which he occupied at 15 Patrick Street.

All of them — the well-known and the nameless rhymesters — are still very much part of the Dublin lore and the traditions which they recorded in their ballads. Their eccentric and colourful outpourings are not merely a haphazard collection of quaint and idle verses for mere entertainment — they are part of the everyday life of the city, part of the accumulated thought which can give a deeper insight into the soul of the citizens. They provide a handy, easily accessible and commonsense guide into the ordinary occurrences of life and a glimpse into remote traditions and happenings. They depict the interests, the humour and the political satires of our ancestors. At their worst they show our vulgar prejudices, and at their best they shed a penetrating light onto the nature of the Irish mind and show the national instinct for the value of words.

It is surely part of the charm, the hallowed antiquity and the usefulness of the ballad that it belongs to no one in particular and yet belongs to all of us. And it is thus that it has been handed down to us, a faded and dog-eared broadsheet, a heritage learnt by the fire-side or in the street, a verse or two overheard in the markets or in the pubs — each expressing something of the thoughts and feelings of our people over the centuries. And what of the long-forgotten ballad-makers? Perhaps their greatest epitaph is that written by another anonymous Dublin scribe: "… They wielded their pens, come weal or woe … courage they praised, cowardice they distained and foolishness they ridiculed."

Vulgar Verse And Variations
Rowdy Rhymes And Rec-im-itations,
Bawdy Ballads And Ancient Airs
Overheard At Country Fairs;
Doleful Dirges, Short Or Long,
Dirty Doggerel, Sacred Song,
'Hay Foot, Straw Foot', 'Ease-Of-Heart'
Garnered, Gleaned At City Mart;
Rhyming Couplet, Queer Quatrain
'Ranty-Poly', Rough Refrain
'Lilli-Bullero', 'Rub-A-Dub-Dub'
Croaking Chorus From The Pub;

'Diddly-Di-Do', 'Riddle-Me-Riddle'
Garramucka, Whistle And Fiddle,
Sailor Shanty, Salt Or Sweet
Skipping Games From Dublin Street:
Mad-Ri-Gal And Merry Tune
Lilt And Lyric, Chaunt and Croon
Odious Odes And Paltry 'Pomes'
From The Factories, From The Homes;
Lullaby, Or Low Lament
Ribald Anthem, Rude Comment
'Up She Rises', And 'Yo-Ho-Ho'
… These Are The Only Songs I Know!

THE WHORE FROM HACKBALL'S CROSS

All the culshies agree that the Rose of Tralee
Was a maiden of fame and renown;
Like Rosie O'Grady, that sweet Irish lady,
And the Star of the old County Down;
Plus the Queen of the Boyne, and the Rose of Mooncoin,
And the Lass with the Delicate Air;
There's the Pride of Gleneen, and my Dark Rosaleen,
Each colleen so pure and so fair,
But from east to the west, surely the best
From Bantry to Carrickmacross
Was that charmer of hearts — the queen of the tarts!
The ould hoor from Hack-a-ball's Cross.

Oh a darlin', a daisy; so fat and so lazy,
With arms like the trunks of a tree
And how she'd confound you, when she got them round you
And planked you right down on her knee;
And you knew you were kissed (when she was half-pissed)
Red lips like big lumps of raw meat
And the scent of her breath — I remember it yet!
Stale porter and putrefyin' teeth.
But we never lost hope that she'd learn to use soap
Or even that new dental floss
Though her clothes were in rags — ah the toast of the hags!
The ould hoor from Hack-a-ball's Cross.

Like a wind-blown rose was the drip from her nose,
A dew drop so fragile and thin,
If it just missed her mouth it still journeyed south
And moistened the warts on her chin.
And no tune was so sweet as the hum from her feet
— That song is still deep in my heart! —
There was no one immune to the way she kept tune
With a burp, then a belch and a fart!
You may sing about Tess, Molly, Nancy and Bess
You may praise little Polly or Floss
But none had a wallop like the County Louth trollop
… The ould hoor from Hack-a-ball's Cross.

FORGIVE AND FORGET
(with apologies to Edwin Hamilton, MA, and his *Dublin Doggerels* of 1877)

"Forgive and forget," you say with a smile,
And I freely agree with your plea;
Though I cannot recall who had forgot
Or if the fault lies with you or with me.
You forget that I'm ever forgiving
(I forgive your forgetting that fact)
But remember, I'm given to lapses
And my memory was never intact.
And if I forgot to forgive you
You gave me as good as you got
You remembered all I'd forgotten
And my forgiveness you quickly forgot.

And remember the little forget-me-not
That once I gave to thee?
You didn't forget to fling that back
Though you forgot what that did to me.
You begged its return; "Forgive me," you cried.
I forgave you — or have you forgot? —
But I couldn't recall just what I had done
With your little forget-me-not.
"Forget it!" you said, through a fresh flood of tears,
(Did that mean forgiveness or not?)
I confess that I cannot remember at all
If you forgave all the things I forgot.

But I forgave you, I remember it well,
Though I could not so quickly forget
That you still recall the things I forgot
While forgetting my forgiveness as yet.
I forgave, I forgive, I've forgotten
(Forgive me, I've never kept score!)
Of the times you forgot my forgiving …
I forgive your forgetting once more.
So "Forgive and forget" you say with a smile —
I'll forgive for as long as I'll live!
But dearest I have to be honest with you
… I forget what I have to forgive!

ECHOES

He that has trod our city's streets
And has heard the tales of old …
Who but he has heard so much
That has so well been told?
And did he listen with willing ear
To ballad and rhyme and song
Then he heard an old town's tale
In the music of the throng.

He that has heard the wild catcalls
And harked to the old nick-name …
Who but he has heard so much
of our follies and our fame?
And did he hear, down through the years,
The doggerels that deride
Then he heard an old town's taunting
At pomposity and pride.

He that has walked the Georgian square
And the old Victorian places …
Who but he has seen so much
Of a city's airs and graces?
And did he view with knowing eye
Such elegance and charm
Then he's walked with Swift and Joyce …
And he's walked it arm-in-arm.

GOUGH'S STATUE

On the night of Sunday, July 23rd, 1957, the statue in Phoenix Park erected to the memory of Sir Hubert Gough (1779–1869) was badly damaged by an explosive charge. Gough, a Limerick man who had served in the British army during the nineteenth century, who had been promoted to the rank of Field-Marshal and elevated to the peerage, and who had distinguished himself on active service in the Peninsular war, South Africa, Puerto Rico, West Indies, Surinam, China and India, was a veritable 'Blimpish-Pukkah-Wallah-Sahib' old Empire-builder of the first water. And presumably it was for this reason that the fine equestrian statue in his honour had been singled out for attack by a few of our own 'blimpish boyohs'.

Certain 'armchair generals' on the fringe of the Republican movement were exultant at this latest 'strike' against the hated British Empire — but for the most part Dubliners of every persuasion and party deplored the mindless vandalism that had just deprived them of one of their familiar landmarks, an equestrian statue in bronze which was reputed to be one of the finest of its class in Europe. Within days of the event an anonymous — and some would say an exceedingly 'tasteless'! — piece of verse appeared on the streets and in the pubs of Dublin condemning this latest desecration of one of our monuments. For those who deprecated the destruction of 'anudder bit of our culture', the lampooning verse was couched in just the appropriate 'cornerboy language' to match the cornerboy vandalism responsible for the mindless act. To others — prudes, puritans and petty nationalists — it was grossly offensive.

In his excellent biography of the late Brendan Behan, Mr Ulick O'Connor attributes the verses to Behan. This is quite understandable, because at the time no one came forward to claim authorship, and as Behan was one of the few people in Dublin in those days with the effrontery to use such four-letter words publicly, and (as Mr O'Connor states in his book) Brendan Behan — while never actually claiming authorship — at the same time never denied it.

But Behan never wrote 'The Ballad of Gough'. That dubious distinction belongs to the present writer. And here, for the first time — with neither pride nor penitence — are the facts of the matter.

On the Monday morning following the damage to the statue in question a group of us machine-room apprentices at Alex Thom, Iona Road, were discussing the matter — or the outrage, depending on how one looked at such things! — just before the 8 o'clock hooter. Naturally there were one or two who were 'thrilled' with the news, though the majority (even those of a more ardently nationalistic frame of mind) condemned it as a senseless act of hooliganism, and in the customary manner of our normal, though not acerbaceous, arguments quite a number of 'apprentice expletives' were tossed back and forth. Later in the morning — during the 10 o'clock teabreak — I scribbled down the words of 'The Ballad of Gough', and incorporated into its verses the recently-heard expletives.

The 'pome' was intended solely for my fellow-apprentices — Jimmy Duffy, Oliver Hoey, Dennis Finn, Frank Casserley, Tommy Kelly, etc. — but in the nature of such things it was passed on to one of the journeymen, Alec Thompson, who then passed it over to some of his caseroom colleagues. By lunchtime the ballad had been set in the Lino-hall and a dozen or so galley pulls taken off old Paddy Murphy's proofing press.

That same evening — Monday being the traditional evening for Chapel Officers from the various Dublin printing offices to attend the weekly Council Meeting at the Dublin Typographical Provident Society offices, 35 Lower Gardiner Street, for the enactment of union business — our Father of the Chapel (I think it was Jimmy Smithers at the time) brought with him a few of the galley pulls and passed them around his colleagues in the council chamber. Those delegates belonging to the night chapels of the four Dublin newspapers — the Indo, the Press, the Times and the Mail — then brought their copies of the ballad to their respective offices, passed them round, and the whole operation was repeated — lino typesetting, clandestine printing on the proofing press — so that there were sufficient copies ready for the 'morning editions' in the market pubs. Similarly with some of their colleagues in the jobbing offices the next day, Tuesday, and by payday of that week there were a couple of hundred 'nixered' broadsheets of the ballad being passed from hand to hand in the boozing kens of the city centre. By the middle of the following week we were hearing reports of 'gestetnered', handwritten, typed and stencilled copies turning up in places as far away as Arklow, Navan and Athlone! An anonymous bestseller — though it never cost, or made, a ha'penny!

And its sudden, though brief, notoriety gave me quite a few anxious moments. My late father — though there was no better man for a joke and a humorous recitation! — strongly disapproved of cornerboy language. (In this regard he was fond of quoting Talleyrand's dictum that "obscenities and vulgarities are the means by which the ignorant give to themselves the semblance of eloquence".) And during the couple of weeks of 'Gough's' popularity my younger brother, Noel (then serving his apprenticeship in my father's hairdressing salon, *The Moorhead*) had to undergo the periodic purgatory of visits from customers — many of them compositors and pressmen from the Indo who were fully aware of the author's identity and his relationship to the *padrone!* — who insisted on quoting odd lines from 'Gough', much to the annoyance of the *padrone* and to the discomfort of his apprentice.

But, thankfully, in the nature of things 'The Ballad of Gough' was quickly forgotten. More than a decade passed before my brothers and I informed the generous-hearted gentleman who was our father just who exactly had written the words of 'Gough'. It happened quite accidentally, when the four of us — the Da, Noel, Jack and meself — were having a pleasant pint in Conway's, and it cropped up quite casually when we were discussing the rapidly changing city that we all loved so much. When we told him, he merely gave that wise, philosophical, Latin shoulder shrug that he had inherited from his Italian grandfather, and he said:

"I think you could have done better, son. At the same time I must admit that no words are strong enough to condemn such vandalism, so I don't blame you. Still, better they blow up statues instead of people, wouldn't you say?"

God bless him. And in some ways I'm glad he's not here today to see some of the things that are happening in Ireland.

'Nuff said! Time for you to read 'The Ballad of Gough' and make up your own mind …

THE BALLAD OF GOUGH

There are strange things done from twelve to one
In the Hollow at Phaynix Park,
There's maidens mobbed and gentlemen robbed
In the bushes after dark;
But the strangest of all within human recall
Concerns the statue of Gough,
'Twas a terrible fact, and a most wicked act,
For his bollix they tried to blow off!

'Neath the horse's big prick a dynamite stick
Some gallant 'hayro' did place,
For the cause of our land, with a match in his hand
Bravely the foe he did face;
Then without showing fear — and standing well clear —
He expected to blow up the pair
But he nearly went crackers, all he got was the knackers
And he made the poor stallion a mare!

For his tactics were wrong, and the prick was too long
(the horse being more than a foal)
It would answer him better, this dynamite setter,
The stick to shove up his own hole!
For this is the way our 'hayroes' today
Are challenging England's might,
With a stab in the back and a midnight attack
On a statue that can't even shite!

WAYZGOOSE*

*"Will ya come to the Chapel Dance?" sez Rent-a-Row to me
And sez I to Rent-a-Row: "Is it goin' to be much of a spree?"
Sez Rent-a-Row with a grin: "Have ya heard of the
Ragman's Ball?
Have ya heard of the Waxies Dargle — well our dance bates
them all!"*

*Sez I to Rent-a-Row: "Where will the hooley be?"
"The Dublin Sports Hotel," sez Rent-a-Row to me.
"Shure how am I to get there, 'cept with a lot of fuss?"
Sez Rent-a-Row a-smilin': "We've ordered a double-deck bus."*

*"And what will the ticket cost?" sez I to Rent-a-Row;
"Thirteen quid the lot — the dance, the band, the chow …
An' a bloody big box o' choc'lates presented to yo'r mot …
Wen'sday twelve December, at nine-ish on the dot."*

*"An' who am I subsidizin'?" I smirks at Rent-a-Row;
"Oh dhivil the subsidizin', let me tell ya the why an' the how …
(And his next words did surprise me — tho' fairly far
from stunned)
"The blokes from '35' are paid from the Chapel Fund."*

*"Fair enough," sez I (though I didn't quite agree)
"'Coz I've heard a bit of a rumour that some of the
folks come free";
"Them is our honoured guests, an' I'd further like to mention
They've earned their honoured place now that they're on pension."*

"*Well that's a daycent gesture,*" *to Rent-a-Row I states,*
"*Fair dues to all the members what don't forget auld mates;*
But I have one final question, if you'll bear with me a while …"
"*Oh fire away, sagosha,*" *he answered with a smile.*

"*Is it fanciful and formal?*" *I next asked Rent-a-Row.*
"*Ah dhivil the bit of formal — more of a 'rowdy-dow' …*
An' dhivil the bit of fancy — more a bit of a farce …
With messers like the Mulvilles, an' Bugsie an' Short-arse.

"*We've Heffo an' Moon an' Liver, the Councillor Lynch as well*
We've the Doc an' Holy Dodd, an' the Garlic Pimpernel,
We'll have singin', we'll have dancin'; and lots o' mots for clickin'
We'll have comps and operators and the likes of the
Wicked Chicken …

We'll have girls in all their fin'ry and fellahs wearin' suits
We'll have gargle be the gallon, we'll have meat an' sweet and
fruits!"
"*Enough! Enough!*" *I quickly cried; "I'll buy me ticket now!*"
"*An' you've made a wise decision,*" *said the man called*
Rent-a-Row.

So me mot is lookin' forward an' she's leppin' at the chance
Of meetin' all me mates at the Chapel Christmas Dance;
Wen'sday is the evenin', and twelve it is the date …
So get your feckin' tickets before you're feckin' late!

* A wayzgoose is a printing fraternity annual dinner or celebration.

THE CONQUERORS

(The historians tell us that within a few generations the
Anglo-Norman invaders had become 'more Irish than the
Irish themselves'.)

When the English robbed our language
And they gave us theirs instead,
They gave us leave to cheat them
In the things we left unsaid;
When they robbed us of our claymores
And thought our pikes absurd
We fashioned brand-new weapons
With each odd, new-fangled word.
For we took the 'ould' King's English
And turned it right around
And perfected 'darlin' phrases
The invader to confound;
And we infiltrated earldoms
Of our Norman overlords
And we overpowered their weapons
With the way we used their words.
When they asked us forthright questions
We responded with a rhyme
And we circumnavigated
Until a better time.
When they grew exasperated
With all this 'faddle-fiddle'
We donned our funny faces
And we posed for them a riddle,
And by the time they'd worked it out
We had drifted far away

To polish up our proverbs
For to 'fight' another day.
We promptly paid the price they asked
Though convincing them indeed
That it was only half the sum
That we first of all agreed;
We vowed we'd neither rob nor cheat …
But nothing said of "diddlin'" …
For nothing's really black nor white
But rather "fair to middlin'"
And when they roarèd and ranted
And said: "That isn't fair!"
We nodded and we answered:
"But that's nayther here nor there!"
And when they tried to fathom out
If this was right or wrong
We'd divert them with a little dance
And regale them with a song,
Or educate them to the fact
That words are all a game
And certain things are better called
By a rather different name,
That just because we use a term
It need not signify
Exactly what it seems to mean —
Though it's neither truth nor lie!
"You're right, milord," we'd loyally cry
"Though it's also truth to tell
That he who says you're wrong, milord,
Is also right as well …

For God would never close one door
Without opening up another —
And everything is something else …
Nayther one thing nor the other!
And God is good, Saint Patrick says,
And the Pope he is our leader …
But then, upon the other hand,
The dhivil's not bad either.
So you see the way it has to be
If we must live together
You must vow to lower the tax
And we'll pray for harvest weather!"
And by the time the Norman lord
Had reckoned we were right
We'd married off our daughters fair
To his reeves and to his knight;
And he was left to ponder:
"Shure, what was all the fuss?
When all is said and done
Aren't they just the same as us?"
And then we urged the Norman lord
To build a monast'ry,
For we told him that the Saviour
Would protect his progeny,
And when we had him on his knees
Convinced he was a sinner
We gently whispered in his ear:
"Now I ask yeh — who's the winner?"

THE FORSAKEN MAIDEN

Oh I am a forsaken maiden
And he was a for'castle tar,
On the foreshore he swore that he loved me
And I forgot he was going too far.
There was none to forearm or forewarn me
To foretell me how to forbid
And I'd not the foresight to forestall him
To foresee that I'd bring forth a kid.

For his forehead was flush to my forelock
And his forearm was forced round my hip
As he fretted and floundered and flustered
And his forefinger fiddled my zip.
Forefending, foregoing, forbidding
My virtue was thrust to the fore
Yet before the forenoon was finished
The aforesaid had made me a whore.

Then he bid fond farewell from the foremast
Went foretop for to set the foresail
While his friends and his fellows foregathered
Fore-and-aft and along the taffrail;
While I followed forlorn on the foreshore
And forthwith I began to forecast
That the curse of his forebears would follow
That foul-hearted wretch up the mast.

For as much as that fecker forsook me
I frothed and fretted, forsooth,
With forebodings of every misfortune
To flatten the philanderin' brute.
That he'd fall when unfurling the foresail
Was my frequent and most fervent wish
That five fathoms deep would he flounder
… And his foreskin make food for the fish!

GLI SCALPELLINI

They came from sunny, vine-clad hills,
or fields that knew the arid drought,
And forever said farewell to homes
Destroyed by despots in the south.
To the grey-damp cities of the north
(Where bitter tears are better lost in rain)
They marched away in dark defeat
Through mists that blurred the shape of pain.

They were artisans and peasant men
From the sun-rich Roman shore
And to a timeless Celtic isle
They brought their ancient lore;
In this alien, green and fertile land
Where famine late held sway
They found a kindred suffering
And they vowed to halt and stay.

They unpacked their age-old secrets
Like peddlers at the fair
And they pointed to the graveyards grey
And the churches gaunt and bare:
And they spoke with simple gestures
Of how they shared a common creed
And the native people nodded
As they sensed the strangers' need.

Then they carved their simple effigies —
The Crucified — The Thief —
And they mingled all their heartbreak
With a hapless nation's grief.
They worked with stone and chisel sharp
With the marble and the tile;
They carved, and cut, and painted …
And with time began to smile.

Then the native notes of wistfulness
Joined their lilting, sunlit songs
And with the sharing and the singing
Each forgot their ancient wrongs.
For they hoisted rough-hewn granite
And they struck with ringing tone
And they hammered out a victory
And composed their hymns in stone.

Many of the Italian immigrants who arrived in Ireland in the middle and latter half of the nineteenth century were stonemasons, church decorators and terrazzo tile workers. A great number of them were political refugees displaced by the

Risorgimento wars and fleeing from the oppressive regimes of the Hapsburgs and the Bourbons.

In Ireland, after the winning of Catholic Emancipation in 1829, there was something of a boom in church building and decoration, and in the decades immediately following the Famine years of 1845–48 there was a considerable demand for ornamental gravestones, family memorials and statuary etc. Italian craftsmen — with names like Pacini, Bassi, Arigho, Nannetti, Caprani, Deghini et al — found not only employment for their skills but a welcoming new homeland.

THE CHANGES

Stroll around your city's streets,
Learn your city's story,
Try to spy the ancient stones —
Those granite-glints of glory —
Or the little stones that seem to hold
All we once held dear —
Before the carpetbaggin' fucks
Make them disappear!

The wattled wall, the lime-washed cot,
The Georgian portico,
Track them down and seek them out
Before they have to go.
View them with a loving eye —
Jewels to fill your gaze! —
Before the gombeen profiteer
Has numbered all their days!

He'll swear there is no other way
That progress asks its price
That heritage is all hogwash
And there is no other choice
That everything is just a slum
"The sooner down, the better,
Besides, I'm covered by the law —
If not the spirit, then the letter!"

No Norman knight, nor English king
Did township so malign
Than that money-grabbing bastard,
Our native philistine!
Bulldozin' things have flattened us
And bullshit is the rule

And even death, the leveller,
Was never half so cruel;
For it took the 'dawn of progress'
And the reign of native raper
To violate our mother town
With erection of skyscraper.

THE DUBLINER

I'm yo'r true-born native Dublin man — not aisy to define,
Save to say, in a prideful way, that I'm from an ancient line.
I boast a noble lineage — I know it off by heart! —
Sir Tristan and Isolde, and King Conaire Mac Art.
For I'm Gael and Norse and Norman stock, and
Huguenot moreover;
I'm Sitric blonde and Strongbow brave, and scion of Danish rover.
I'm Palatine (came from the Rhine), I'm Fleming and Walloon;
I'm soldier, sailor, jarvey, tailor; I'm pikeman and dragoon.
I'm a weaver from the Liberties, a sawyer from Portobell-a,
I'm a butcher boy from Ormond Quay, I'm a rag-and-bones
'oul fellah';
I'm the olive-skinned Eye-talian man that invented
'wan-and-wan'
Or the Hebrew hawkin' haberdash from dawn 'till setting sun.
I'm Tiger Roche and Zozimus, I'm Billy-in-the-Bowl;
I'm pinkadindie, latchiko — and the true 'heart of the rowel'.
I'm 'relationed' to the Twangman's mot, I've cousins one and all
That drank their fill at Finnegan's Wake, likewise the
Ragman's Ball.

I've trawled for herrings in the bay, and sold them from a cart,
I've kissed the hand of Moll Malone, but couldn't win her heart.
I'm also kin to Skin-the-Goat that spurned the Saxon shillin'
(Could not be bought, wore convict cloth, before he'd act
the villain!)

From Waterloo to 'Bastapol I've charged the foreign snipers
And left me blood on distant soil from Colenso down to 'Wypers';
At Easter Week I reached me peak, in my own native town
Though cannon blazed it took five days before they wore us down!
Thus Fusilier or Volunteer as the mood or memory rouses —
Yet a peaceable lar that likes a jar (so a curse on both their
houses!).
And I've drawn the dole, and hefted coal, with Whacker,
Jem and Ned
And I've carried hods and stacked the sods upon the Featherbed.
From Ray-town out to Ballybough, and 'tween the two canals,
I've worked and toiled, I've kipped and moiled, with staunch
and loyal pals.
From Harolds Cross I've pitched and tossed to Alexander's Basin
From day to day I've earned me pay with docker and with mason.
From Brazen Head to Monto town my wheel turns on its hub
And I draw my pride from Liffey side because I am a Dub!
So when the Judgement day is nigh, and I slip this mortal coil
No Gabriel's horn will sound that morn to salute my days of toil
No angels' choir will thus inspire, or sing my race is run
'Cause I'll proudly wait at the pearly gate for a 'toot' from the
'Bugler' Dunne!

Tiger Roche: an eighteenth-century 'character', leader of a gang of
street ruffians and 'harum-scarums' known as the Mohawks.

Zozimus: Michael Moran, born in Faddle Alley in 1794, and one of Dublin's best-known and prolific ballad-makers.

Billy-in-the-Bowl: Another eighteenth-century 'character', a legless ex-soldier (?) who propelled himself about the streets by means of his massive arms and shoulders, the stumps of his thighs protected from the pavements and rough cobblestones by resting in a padded, shallow basket, or 'bowl', which was held in place by leather straps suspended from his shoulders, back and front.

'Before passing away from Grangegorman the story, as narrated by Burton, of "Billy in the Bowl" must not be omitted. This character used to ply his calling between the quiet streets of Stoneybatter and the Green Lanes of Grangegorman. He was nicknamed "Billy in the Bowl," having been introduced into the world with only a head, body, and arms. When he grew up he conveyed himself along in a large bowl fortified by iron, in which he was embedded. This man was the original "Billy in the Bowl," for though many other personages who got along in various ways were honoured with the same sobriquet, yet this fellow was the king of them all. He soon ingratiated himself with the simple servant maids from Meath in the respectable houses of Oxmantown. "It's only Billy in the Bowl, ma'am." "Oh, very well," and Billy's bowl was filled with beef, bread, etc. Nature had compensated for his curtailment by giving him fine dark eyes, an aquiline nose, and a well-formed mouth, with dark curling locks, and a body and arms of herculean power. It was not to be wondered at, therefore, that hearts susceptible to pity should be touched by the peculiar circumstances of this *lusus naturae.* He certainly won the hearts of the plebeian fair north of the Liffey. Amongst them he was a universal favourite. It had, nevertheless, transpired in sober circles that Billy in the Bowl had been suspected of very atrocious deeds. He was one of those curious beggars who frequented fairs and public places, where he picked up a good deal of money. The manner in which it is said he committed his depredations was by secreting himself in a ditch or inside a hedge on a lonely part of the road or unfrequented corner till a suitable person was passing on whom he might practice, and then, addressing them in a plaintive strain, begged of them to assist a poor, helpless man. They, struck by his peculiar circumstances, stepped aside to view the strange sight — half-man, half-bowl — and were soon undone in one way or another. It is said he murdered his victims; otherwise so marked a man would soon have been detected had they escaped to denounce him. But his visits to Oxmantown and its environs at last ceased in consequence of his failure in attempted robbery of two ladies who were passing through what was then known as Richardson's Lane, now a portion of the Royal Barracks (prison side), when at one of the stiles or passages between the fields they saw Billy in his bowl. The unsuspecting ladies were by no means displeased at the *recontre*, the female curiosity, together with Billy's coaxing ways, induced them to draw near to examine how he was disposed in his extraordinary vehicle, resolving in the humanity of their hearts to give him something. They both expressed their admiration and pity, whilst Billy was profuse in his commendation of the "fine ladies" who had so "marcifully" come out of their way to see the "poor prisoner". One of them was applying her eye-glass to inspect more perfectly Billy's premises, and the other was preparing her gratuity to drop into his bowl. The fellow's eyes were gloating in the meantime on their gold watches, bracelets, and other valuable trinkets which the ladies of that period were ornamented with, when, watching his opportunity, the base fellow attacked them, and, before they could think what was the matter, dragged them down. Their confusion, and the destruction of their habiliments, together with the rude efforts the villain was making to possess himself of their valuables, at first rendered them powerless; they, however, began at last to struggle and call for help; but, alas, none was then near. The ruffian was endeavouring to shove his heavy bowl over one, till he had robbed the other lady, yet with all his strength, the defect of his lower man gave the unfortunate females an advantage. One seized his curling locks with her hand, whilst she contrived to thrust her thumb into one of Billy's eyes. The fellow roared with pain, and relaxed his hold of the other lady, who sprang up, disordered as she was. They now contrived to get out of his range, but in a most soiled and tattered condition — their hair dishevelled, their ornaments broken and scattered, clothes ruined — whilst Billy himself, almost deprived of the sight of one of his eyes, was left in his bowl to lament his wretched situation, and the certain punishment that awaited him. The poor gentlewomen returned to their friends in Manor Street, and having told their story, no time was lost in pursuing the wretch who had committed such an assault. Billy, in the meantime, had contrived to screen himself behind a hedge in the next field, but was soon detected, most of the valuables were picked up on the ground where the attack had taken place, and some of the party procured a strong hand-barrow, on which Billy was conveyed in triumph to prison. (It was just about this time, 1786, that a police force was established in Dublin.) Billy was confined in the jail in Green Street, where as much of him as could be made use of was employed in hard labour for the remainder of his days. In consequence of this fellow's ill-fame, and the audacious feats he had performed, he became the object of great curiosity, and was visited as one of the "lions of the day". (*Life in Old Dublin,* James Collins, Tower Books, Cork [Reprint] 1978)

Pinkindindie: eighteenth-century 'pinker' or cutpurse.

Latchiko: (origin uncertain); dockland slang for 'waster' or rogue.

Skin-the-Goat: James Fitzharris, the Dublin jarvey whose coach was used by the 'Invincible' conspirators, and which conveyed them to Phoenix Park for the purpose of assassinating the Chief Secretary, Lord Frederick Cavendish, and the Under-Secretary, Mr Burke, in July 1882. Fitzharris was apprehended as an accomplice and sentenced to fifteen years hard labour for his adamant refusal to point out the actual assassin or assassins, despite the offer of a substantial cash reward, a new identity for himself and his family and free transportation to one of the colonies should he act as a crown witness. On his release from prison in the early years of the last century, and in poor health, he obtained employment for a time as a Corporation watchman, or 'gotchy', in the East Wall area (largely through the efforts of William T. Cosgrave, then a city councillor), and he died before the 1914–18 War. Some years ago his granddaughter informed me that even on his deathbed he refused to divulge the name of the actual assassin to members of his own family; with what were virtually his last words he closed the chapter on the 'Phoenix Park Murders' and the Invincibles with the statement: "I've kept this secret for so long, and I've suffered for it, that it's best now if I take it to the grave with me.'

'Fitzharris, an ugly, whiskery, jaunty, picturesque figure in a shabby black overcoat, a jarvey's waistcoat, and a red neckerchief … a coarsely cheerful, robust and elderly man, well-known to Dubliners as "Skin-the-Goat" because of a tale about his selling the hide of a pet animal to pay for his drinking debts.' *(The Phoenix Park Murders,* Tom Corfe, Hodder and Stoughton, 1968)

'A poorly dressed old man passed the time of day with my uncle and I was told, as if it were a great secret, that the man was "Skin-the-Goat", the jarvey who drove the Park murderers. I got a confused picture of Carey the Informer, Joe Brady, and a knife. "Skin-the-Goat", whose real name was Fitzharris, lived in lower Rutland Street and whenever he passed, people nudged one another and said "there's Skin-the-Goat". I don't think he was ostracised, but people were not too anxious to be seen talking to him. Despite all the hysterical public denunciation of the Park murders, the common people of Dublin hated the memory of Carey the Informer, who betrayed the conspirators, and had a not so sneaking admiration for Joe Brady, the youngest of the conspirators. My tribal prejudices were being created and the tribal folklore absorbed.' *(Dublin Made Me, An Autobiography,* C. S. Andrews, The Mercier Press, 1979)

Bugler Dunne: The fifteen-year-old boy hero of the Boer war. During the crossing of the Tugela river in December 1899, and in the confusion caused by a surprise attack by the Boers, what might have been a disastrous rout for the British forces was turned into a partial victory by the bugler sounding 'Advance' instead of 'Retreat', as he had been instructed to do. When questioned later by superior officers the boy naively stated that, as it was his very first time under fire, he naturally took the order to be one of 'Advance' because his father (a career soldier and a sergeant in the Dublin Fusiliers) had always told him that the 'Fusiliers never retreat'.

Dunne was later decorated, received at Buckingham Palace by the ageing Queen Victoria, and then toured the British music halls with his 'bugle act' as part of a British army recruitment campaign. He served again in the Great War, was later a seaman, and died in his native Dublin in the 1950s.

Chaunt: (page 9) 'Chaunting would appear to have been a some-what nauseating distortion of the modern presentation of a recitative (a monologue, half sung, half spoken), usually of some of the most frightful doggerel ever to fall from the pen of the pseudo-poet, of which there appear to have been many ... These doggerel chaunts of the taverns of Regency London reflect a social and communal atmosphere which is at once strange and indefinable. They illumine nothing but the appalling ignorance and abysmal mental under-nourishment of those unenlightened days.' *(Strange Encounters,* James Brady, Hutchinson, London, 1946)

THE SHAWLIE

One rarely sees a shawlie these days. Changing times and changing fashions have at last put paid to their presence. A pity. As the name implies, a 'shawlie' was one of those little old women — or oul' wans — habitually enveloped in a big black shawl and who used to frequent the Dublin streets, churches, markets and pubs right up until the early 1960s. Alas, they are no more.

The shawlie was essentially a kind-hearted, motherly, garrulous — and very occasionally a vituperative! — granny who stoutly defended old decency and every truant schoolboy and street urchin who happened to run foul of schoolmasters, policemen, stall-holders or cinema ushers. "Lave your hand off the poor child for goodness sake! Shure what harm is he doin' pinchin' an oul' apple and him half starved and near fallin' down dead with the hunger! Were you never a child yourself? Let go of him this minnit ya big bully!"

The lash of her tongue saved many of us from a trashing. And her gentler tones and the fringe of her shawl wiped away many of our tears. When we grew to manhood it was our wont — as much for the entertainment value of her discourses as from any notions of plebeian chivalry — to buy a jar or two for any old shawlie found sitting alone in the quiet corner of a pub. The money was invariably well spent, for the shawlie's speech usually ran something like this:

"Ah, the blessings of God on you son for the drink! May you slip into Heaven ten minnits before the divil knows you're dead! I don't mind tellin' you that I was in dire need of a drop just now, 'cause I've just come from the chapel and me poor throat is worn to sandpaper from the heap of rosaries that I said for the deceased.

Did you not know him? The second oul' fellah to drop dead out of our street this week. First there was a man in Number Twelve last Tuesday. And now Number Seventeen. The green hall door and the peelin' paint. Lord have mercy on him. Ah you remember him, don't you? Oul' Onion-Sack Byrne, they called him. A little bockety, bunty, baldy, bandy class of a man. Well, not exactly baldy. More of a retrievin' hairline. And not really bandy either, though there was an awful immensity of ground between his knees. Yeah, well he's the one. Number Seventeen. Green hall door and dirty curtains.

Hey, come here. Will I tell you what I think? I think he was murdered. And I think she done it. Are me lips movin'? I don't want anyone to know what I'm whisperin' to you. But I think she done it. She's goin' round tellin' everyone that he died of a massive crow-nary on account of the varico veins and since the ballinx of his mind was disturbed due to him bein' depressed after he was made repugnant from the job.

Depressed, him? Shure only last week he was waddlin' around as happy as a lamb with the two mammies. And now look at him, God help him — a free night in the chapel all to himself and covered in flowers.

I'd say she definitely done it. I mean, she's been promisin' to do him in for years. Made no secret of it. And you can't blame her, can you? I don't. Ah no, there's no bloody way I'd put the blemt on her. Livin' all them years with Oul' Onion-Sack must've made the Crucifixion of Our Lord look like a nixer — comin' home every night in the small hours of the mornin' with a bellyful of cold porter and if he wasn't demandin' his congenital rights he was usin' her as a punch bag, God help her. Oh, every night! Wham, slam, bam! whether or which.

And she was worse, arguin' back at him instead of traipsin' down to the Well Battered Woman's Centre or the Rape Crisis place — you know, where they give out all them Protestant counter-ceptives and abortment pills. Poor Mrs Onion-Sack could've used a few of them abortment pills, and no mistake. Would've done her a power of good. Twelve, she had. Like steps of stairs, one after the other. Oh, he was a beast for you know what. Hey, come here — maybe that's what killed him? What do you think?

Still and all, I'm against them abortments. I mean to say, to think of four thousand Irish girls goin' over to pagan England every year and gettin' that done. Disgraceful, that's what it is. Why can't they stay at home and give all that work to Irish doctors? It's not a bit Catholic or patriotic. But shure the nature isn't in the young wans anymore. And poor Mrs Onion-Sack should've gotten a historical-ectomy years ago. It's a woman's operation where they remove the carry-cot and leave you with the play-pen, so to speak.

Anyway, as I was sayin' — I think she done him in. 'Cause he was always thumpin' her. My fellah, God be good to his blessed memory, used to say that it's often that a person's mouth can break his nose, and that poor craythur in Number Seventeen with the green hall door had her nose broken as often as her heart. Up and down to Jervis Street Hospital every second week for a nostril transplant. I don't know how she put up with it. Ah, God love her, she was always soft-hearted.

I'd say she done it alright. Poisoned his porter, most likely. Painless. Pityin' him right at the end and givin' him the pleasure of his pint and polishin' him off all at the same time. And I wouldn't be a bit surprised if she died of a broken heart herself next week. It would be just like her to go out in symphony with him. She's that sort really, hatin' him and lovin' him all at the same time. 'Course we're all the same, aren't we? We are, people is only human bein's.

The nature is in us you see, and we're too misfortunate for our own good, thank God ..."

THE SHAWLIE

You can see her beyond in the snug
Wrapped in her ould black shawl,
Whisperin' softly to herself
And mindin' no one a-tall,
For her thoughts 'ill be turnin' inwards
And she'll nod her head awhile
At the pull of the ould time mem'ries
That lend sadness to her smile.

She'll sip at her glass of porter
Prolongin' the dark delight
And tastin' the stored-up mem'ries
That must last her through the night
As she peers at the rearward livin'
And the years that have taken their toll —
Just one o' them darlin' ould-wans
That have given our town its soul.

So let's buy her a bottle o' Guinness
Or a glass of the warmer stuff,
A drop of the 'how's-yor-father'
To go with her pinch of snuff.
We'll be rewarded ten times over
With a smile that's second to none
And an age-old benediction …
"Ah the blessin's o' God on yeh, son!"

THE IRISH HOOR

("There was no sex in Ireland before television" —
the late Oliver Flanagan, TD, talking to Gay Byrne on 'The
Late Late Show')

*In the Land of the Saints and the Scholars licentiousness never
was known,*
In the four fertile fields of old Erin never the wild oats were sown;
*No 'laying', no 'screwing', no 'scoring', no piece on the side and
no crumpet;*
*In the tongue of the Gael from the past you'll find ne'er a
mention of 'strumpet'.*
*No harems, no brothels, no 'kip-shops' did sully the land of
the Celt*
No wife-swapping bed-hopping antics, no need for a chastity belt,
*Where virtue indeed was triumphant and the Round Tower
alone was erect*
*(Resembling a great phallic symbol, did the saints and the
scholars suspect*
*That the towers that embellished the landscape, standing in
grandeur and pride*
*Would open the doors of conjecture for the smut-minded
students of Freud?)*

*Thus eschewing the sins of the flesh we fashioned the purest
of nations,*
*A land that was emptied of lust, untrammelled by
lewd fornications,*
*No children were born out of wedlock, no coupling by chance or
by proxy,*

In the tongue of the Gael from the past there's ne'er a
translation for doxy.
Nor 'prostitute', 'mistress' or 'call girl', only maidens so chaste
and so pure,
With result that we rendered redundant the trade and the term
of a 'whore'.
We banished the bawd and the tart, as St Patrick once did with
the snake,
And we took to the drink with a vengeance, concupiscence thus
to forsake;
And as proof of our proudest contention — a boast that shall
ever endure!
We're the only people on earth that refer to a man as 'yeh hoor'!

THE OLD MAN IN THE CORNER

(Ballad)

The golden stuff was flowing
And the lounge was warm with light,
And the tinkle-talk of 'cheese-and-wine'
Echoed softly through the night;
And they talked of Costa Brava
And how the wife now needs a car,
Of games of golf, and pension plans
As they leaned against the bar.

But the old man in the corner
Just slowly shook his head
"I was with Jem Larkin"
Were the only words he said.

His little words were whispered things
And very quickly drowned
In the slap-of-back and laughter
As someone called a round
Then regaled his jolly fellows
With a tale of missing Mass,
And 'having something on the side'
And the latest 'piece of ass'.

But the old man in the corner
Just slowly shook his head
"I was with Jem Conn'ly"
Were the only words he said.

As they sipped their Remy Martins
They began to curse their fate
'All those Welfare wasters!'
'And the heavy interest rate'
And how they'd lost a bundle
At Leopardstown last week;
Or the country needs a Franco
To divide the strong from meek.

But the old man in the corner
Just slowly shook his head
"I was out in 'Thirteen'"
Were the only words he said.

Then a round of double brandies
To toast 'the good old days';
And the old man standing up
To meet each single gaze:
"Good old days be damned!" he cried
"When the choice for the likes of me
Was a starvin' death and a lonesome death
From the scourge of the old TB."

And the old man walked among them
And proudly raised his head
"I was with Noel Browne"
Were the final words he said.

FAMINE

There was hunger in the West
In the year the 'taties died
There was sorrow in my heart
At the way my father cried,
There was suffering and sadness
And a grief beyond my years —
There was vengeance in my heart
When I saw my mother's tears.

Oh the 'big house' kept the barley
And his lordship held the oats
While the tenants trudged on downwards
For to catch the Yankee boats.

There was anquish in my heart
When they laid my parents low
There was terror in my thoughts
When the neighbours bid me go
There was heartbreak in my hiding
Of my tears in Granny's shawl
'Fore the uncles wrenched me townwards
For to catch a Boston yawl.

Oh the 'big home' kept the barley
And his lordship held the oats
While the tenants trudged on downwards
For to catch the Yankee boats.

And the sadness hasn't lessened
With the course of fifty years
And the new land wasn't big enough
To lose my store of tears;
And of late I keep remembering
The things that I loved best
In the year before the taties died
… And our cabin in the West.

Oh the 'big house' kept the barley
And his lordship held the oats
While the tenants trudged on downwards
For to catch the Yankee boats.

THE SAILOR FROM RINGSEND

I think the best of all the old 'rec-im-itations' over the past seventy years or so — certainly one of the most popular — is *The Sailor from Ringsend*, composed by the late Paddy Kenny during the 'Emergency' and the days of wartime shortages and food rationing. Paddy, a fellow printer and a great 'friend o' the family', was not only a talented and versatile stage performer in his own right, but also a dab-hand at the scriptwriting. He wrote numerous gags, sketches, skits, parodies and recitations for (and frequently in conjunction with) such legendary troupers as Cecil Sheridan, Jack Cruise and Arthur Lucan of 'Old Mother Riley' fame.

At my 'journeyman lash-in' (held in McGowan's of the Broadstone in 1958) Paddy was kind enough to compliment me on my rendering of *The Sailor from Ringsend*, and, as one of my printing 'godfathers' — which is to say a sponsor or nominator in the old closed shop days who was instrumental in obtaining an apprenticeship for someone — he made me a present of the following parody with the words:

"Fair play to you, son — you did *The Sailor* proud. And it's my little present to you now that you are 'out of your time'. I give it to you with a heart and a half, and you may use it wherever you like, whenever you like."

As a tribute to one of the great rhymesters I would like to use it now, and to complement and enhance my own pieces by including it among the 'Rowdy Rhymes and Rec-im-itations'.

THE SAILOR FROM RINGSEND

There's a green and yellow dairy to the north of Dolphin's Barn
There's a dairy maid whose heart will never mend;
Every night behind the counter you can hear her tell the yarn
How she loved and lost the sailor from Ringsend.

She was known as Cock-eyed Kate to the lads from James's Gate,
She was hotter than her oul-wan ever knew;
Every night after dark, in the Hollow of the Park
She'd a gang o' fellahs waiting in a queue!

Oh she loved the lads all right, and there seldom was a night
That with one of them she didn't have a bend,
'Till at last there came the day when true love had its way —
Shure she met and loved the sailor from Ringsend.

Kate and he became engaged (though the other fellows raged!)
And her mother — Mrs Anastasia Mary Dooley —
Said she'd give the boys a treat, so she pawned the bedroom suite
And in honour of the day she threw a hooley.

Now the sailor from Ringsend was a true and loyal friend,
Unselfish, as he was hale and hearty,
So in quite heroic fashion he saved up his weekly ration
And he sent a pound of sugar to the party.

On the evening of the spree he was so full up with glee
That he did a thing he knew was very risky
With another gang of looneys he went down the town to Mooneys
And there consumed about a quart of whiskey.

Though the 'do' was not 'till ten, he had not arrived by then
(He spent an hour sortin' out a Bobby!)
And when he arrived late he found his Cock-eyed Kate
With her arms around a milkman in the lobby!

In a frenzy of distress he picked up the kitchen press
Around the milkman's neck he wrapped the delph!
And when Kate saw all this happen, she knew he'd caught her nappin'
And she flew into an awful rage herself.

Though her countenance grew paler she flared up at the sailor:
"I hope that you get shipwrecked in the Mersey!
Take back your diamond ring, from now on I'll have my fling —
And yeh can shove your bag of sugar up your jersey!"

When the sailor got the bird, ah he never said a word,
But he swore he'd be revenged upon the tart;
He stayed on at the party making love to Mags McCarthy
While poor Cock-eyed Kate sat eating out her heart.

And later on at three, when the guests were having tea
The sugar bag he handed to her Ma
She gladly took the bag — the poor ould silly hag —
And she used the stuff to sweeten up the 'cha'.

The guests all drank their teas — but they were soon upon their knees!
In agony they rolled around the room,
And poor Cock-eyed Kate got flummoxed, when she saw them grab their stomachs
For she knew at last that she had met her doom.

With faces gaunt and grey the guests all dashed away
Poor Cock-eyed Kate was left without a friend;
For he'd switched the bag of sugar for a bloody bag of glauber
… 'Twas the vengeance of the sailor from Ringsend!

THE PRIZEFIGHTER'S PRAYER

There were two old fighters who were familiar sights around the O'Connell Street and centre city area back in the late 1940s and early 1950s — 'Cyclone' Billy Warren (an American negro who had married an Irish woman and who lived somewhere up around the Nelson Street district) and Mike Farrell (a tough-as-nails little Galway man who had been dubbed by world champion Al McCoy as 'the toughest of the whole mob').

'Cyclone' Warren used to stand outside the old Metropole (now Penney's beside the GPO) for most of the day, a quiet, stooped, soulful-looking man in a bowler hat and a faded Crombie topcoat, and then, in the evening, he would shuffle homewards on tired old feet, his *malacca* cane helping him as he wheezed slowly along. Mike Farrell also used a cane — for the second old-timer was totally blind as a result of injuries received in the ring — but he was straight-shouldered and 'chin-up' as he tap-tapped his way from the Richmond Institute for the Blind (now the Royal Dublin Hotel) to either of the two Parnell streets, up to Bob Kearney's Barber Shop for his haircut and shave, or down and round the corner to Mooney's for a glass of his favourite beverage, barley wine.

The two old fighters were friends, and it was a friendship that went back over nearly half a century — back to the night when they first encountered each other in the hostile territory of a roped square at the Lennox Athletic Club, New York City around 1909. And therein lies a little story which Mike Farrell once recounted to me over a jar in the same Mooney's of Parnell Street:

"Cyclone Billy was a real genul'man. Damn fine scrapper too, though when I fought him he was gettin' on a bit and well past his best. Yeh see, Vince, Billy Warren had been through all them 'battle royals' round the turn of the century. Ever hear of them? No — well, yeh see, these here 'battle royals' was when some smart-ass promoter fella would shove about a half dozen of these big nigger guys inta the ring — all at the same time, mind ye — and then let the lot of them lambaste each other for ould divarshun. Last man standin' collected the purse money. Real rough stuff, it was. 'Course, often as not, the guys would arrange to split the cash between 'em afterwards in the alley, 'cause they was mostly hungry. But no matter which way yeh look at it those black guys had ta work real hard for their dinner. An' like I was sayin', Billy Warren was one of them veterans. Tough.

Gave me some hard moments durin' our match, I can tell yeh — him bein' a natural middle, a lot taller than me, with a longer reach an' a damn eddicated pair o' mitts — an' for them first few rounds I was like a cat in a tripe shop, not knowin' which end to tackle first. But Billy was gettin' on a bit in years, an' the ould legs was startin' to give out, so that I fin'lly caught up with him around the seventh and floored him. Left hook, then a right — wham, wham! Down he went like an empty sack. He got up once, very wobbley, and then I finished him off. The full count. That was that.

Anyways, some time afterwards Cyclone Billy comes to Europe while I stays on in the States. Yeh see, them black fellahs was allus pop'lar in France in them years — Johnson, Langford, Joe Jeanette, MacVeigh — they could allus make a bit of cash and they usually got a better deal than in the States. Same in England, I believe. Cyclone Billy had a few fairly good years and then he came to Dublin 'round the time of that first big war with the Germans. I believe he had a couple o' fights here, though I'm none too sure on that score 'cause they tell me that there was a kinda rebellion goin' on here at the time, an' let's face it, people is on'y human bein's an' there's no damn way they're goin' ta pay good money in ta see two fist fighters when all they gotta do is look out their own front winda's to see a real fight, with guns and bombs an' all, for free.

Well anyway, 'round the time Cyclone Billy came here he was buttonholed by a couple of newspaper guys an' he gave them a story about how in over a couple o' hunnard contests he was never once knocked out by nobody. Now that wasn't strictly true, as I've just told yeh, but I can't really say as how I blame Billy. I mean, when you're tryin' ta earn fight money yeh can't go around sellin' yourself short, can yeh?

In the mean whiles I'm still out in the States, makin' good money an' gettin' all the matches I need. In a dozen years I had over three hunnard fights — three hunnard an' sixty at least! — an' I traded thumps with five world champeens, McCoy, Johnny Wilson, Mike O'Dowd, Mick McTeigue and Gene Tunney and not one of 'em ever knocked me out. Not one, in over three hunnard contests! An' yeh gotta remember that I never tipped the scales at much more than one-forty pounds an' still I was goin' in against welters, middles and some of the lightheavies. Jeez, when I fought Tunney I was givin' away twenty pound an' I was already blind in one eye, yet still I went the whole ten rounds with that guy.

Anyway, finally my glims were doused an' I could see nuthin' an' I had to hang up me gloves, an' as there was nuthin' for me in the States anymore I packed up an' came home. That was about twen'nyone or twen'nytwo. I know, 'cause all them Black-an'-Tan guys were packin' up an' headin' home an' our own mob was takin' over.

I'm on'y home a few weeks an' who should bump inta me in the street on'y Cyclone Billy, an' him more of a natchural-ised Dublin man than meself.

'Mike,' sez he, 'Willya do an ole pal a favour?'

'Sure,' sez I, 'just name it.'

'Wal, Mike, it's this way — folks hereabouts reckon I was a fairly important fighter back in the States, kinda like Johnson or Langford, an' I gotta bit of respect in this town. An' I sorta tole 'em that I ain't never been knocked-out by nobody, know what I mean? So Mike, would ya promise an ole buddy that yeh ain't never goin't ta blow the whistle on me an' tell how ya once stiffened me. Promise?"

I promised. Gave Billy me word an' me hand on it. An' that was our own private little secret — sorta private little joke, yeh might say — for the best part o' thirty years. I never spilled on him — save once, an' as God is my judge I swear ta yeh that it wasn't really my blemt!

Yeh see, Vince, it was this way: one night, couple o' years back, I was in here — this very table, if I'm not mistaken—an' havin'a quiet drink when in walks two newspaper guys an' they give me the sad news that Ol' Cyclone Billy is in the hospital an' that these two guys would like some details about him, about his fights an' all that kinda stuff, on account of how they're expectin' my ole pal to be a funeral case — what d'yeh call it, a 'bituary notice or somethin'?

So I tell 'em all I know an' I make damn sure to give Billy a good 'write-up' — yeh know, makin' him sound like he's prob'ly the best ever black boxer next ta Johnson or Langford — an' all the time these two guys are buyin' me a few drinks an' I'm enjoyin' talkin' about the ole days an' me tongue is flappin' away faster than the ould brain — well, yeh gotta remember that I took a helluva lot o' punches ta the head in my time, an' then with all that drink an' all — anyways, the next thing I know I'm suddenly blabbin' out how I was the on'y guy ever to flatten Cyclone Billy. Jeez, I could-a bit me tongue off!

'Course before those guys can mark these words down in their notebooks I'm tellin' them how I promised Billy never to let on about that fight an' I'm makin' it good an' clear that they don't have permission to print that stuff in their papers. They gave me their say-so on it and mouthed a lotta stuff about 'respectin' your wishes' an' 'strickly offa the record' and not to be worryin' about it. So I didn't, an' we had anudder few glasses an' a bit more chat about the ol' days in the fight game, an' that was that.

Next day I gotta friend o' mine that owns a car to drive me to this hospital an' to find me the ward where they're keepin' my ole sparrin' partner. 'Course, on account of me bein' blind I can't see Billy lyin' there in the bed an' I can't tell what sort o' shape he's in, but I sure enough know from the kinda whisperin' way he's talkin' that it's on'y goin' to be a matter of hours.

'Mike,' sez he, 'yeh let me down. Yeh went an' told those newspaper guys how ya stiffened me. That's below the belt, Mike.'

'What d'yeh mean, Billy?' sez I.

'I knows your peepers are gone Mike an' that yeh can't see ta read, an' I'm sure as hell sorry for yeh on that score — but it's all there in today's paper how yeh once pole-axed Cyclone Billy. Now why for did yeh wanna go doin' a low-down thing like that on an ole pal, Mike. Why?'

What could I say?

Tell yeh somethin' for nuthin', Vince — I cried there an' then. Front of all them nurses and patients, an' everyone. Jeez!

An' I'll tellya somethin' else — I got roarin' drunk that same night an' I got this friend o' mine with the car to drive me round all the pubs where all them bastardin' newspaper guys hang out! I tried to bate the bejaysus out of every goddam one of 'em — just walked straight in an' said 'd'yeh work in the papers?' an' if the answer was 'yes' I just fuckin'-well let fly with both fists!

As it turned out me friend with the car had ta get the cops 'cause I was layin' inta every one an' anythin' I could touch, an' half wreckin' some bar — I think it was the Metro, though I can't be sure — an' then a daycent big cop name o' Tom Glackan an' a few of his boys from Fitzgibbon Street station finally took me in hand, though not without a real slugfest. Give them their due they didn't press charges or nuthin' on account of the night that was in it — the night poor old Cyclone Billy passed away."

And that's the truth. Ask Sergeant Tom Glackan.

And Mike himself passed on about 1962.

He was a real 'good un', was Mike Farrell. Despite the dull, sightless eyes, the flattened nose and the squiggles of scar tissue lacing his eyebrows, Mike had a genial, expressive face. He also had a heart of gold. Once, in his cups, he confessed to me that throughout his long and eventful ring career he had never stepped into the ring before a contest without saying a prayer for himself and his opponent.

At first I used to tease 'the toughest of the whole mob' about his prayerful pugilism but gradually I came to respect his evident sincerity and in a rare moment of confidentiality I elicited from him the form and nature of his private prayer. He went into some detail about his thoughts in the dressing room before a contest and when he had finished he directed me to — "write all them words down, Vince. An' then put them inta one o' your pomes — give them a fancy sound, like a real prayer, or a hymn, or somethin'. Okay?"

Here then, is Mike Farrell's prayer. The thoughts, the warm impulse, the philosophy, the spiritual content — call it what you will — are Mike's, the outpourings of a noble, if rough-and-ready, soul. Only the feeble words and the meagre rhyme, which try to give them a 'fancy sound', are mine. Okay, Mike?

THE PRIZEFIGHTER'S PRAYER

I ask You not for victory …
For somehow, that seems wrong,
But only for protection
And the courage to be strong;

Strength — not to conquer —
But just that I'll fight well
And prove myself a sportsman
At the final bell.

I ask you, Christ of Suffering,
That should I suffer pain
I'll offer it for all my sins
So that it won't be in vain.

And if, perhaps, he cuts me
And the bright red blood I see,
I ask that I'll remember
The blood You shed for me.

I need you in my corner,
But likewise, in the other,
So that I'll remember
My opponent is my brother.

And I pray that You'll protect us
From injuries severe,
That we'll give the fans their value
And every cause to cheer.

And make each single act
Of either one be fair,
So no matter who the victor
In the glory both can share.

And if, by chance, he floors me
And the canvas I should meet
Like Simon of Cyrene
Please help me to my feet.

Then should a little glory
Somehow fall on me
Please help me to remember
That I owe it all to Thee.

Please help me go the distance
Through rounds with danger rife
Not only in the boxing square
But in the larger ring of Life.

So I ask You not for Victory …
For somehow, that seems wrong,
But only for protection
And the courage to be strong.

Strength of mind and body
So I'll fight each battle well
And the Referee will raise my hand
At the Judgement's Final Bell.

AND WHO ARE WE TO JUDGE?

There are those whom all the world extols
And those whom we despise,
The first, we credit them with Truth,
The rest, we deem them liars;

The first are on the side of Right
They're noble and they're pure;
The others on the side of Wrong —
The criminal and the whore.

And so we draw a simple line
Betwixt what's wrong and right.
And we learn to make a simple choice
Between the Black and White.

The barons of the Daily Press
And the pulpit-thumping priest
All help our ready-reckoning
Of the 'mighty' and the 'least';

But the printed page may tell a lie
In its haste to hang a man,
(And I've seen the bulge of belly-greed
Beneath the black soutane!)

For silken gowns are splendid things
To shroud a vice within,
While a poor man's tattered shirt
Can scarce conceal his sin.

And I've seen a hint of holiness
In a harlot's helpless guile,
And I've spied the glint of lust
In a Pharisaic smile.

So I do not wish to be a judge —
For I've troubles of my own! —
And Jaysus knows I'd never wish
To cast the sharpest stone.

I'm colour-blind 'twixt black and white
Don't know where to draw the lines
Between the good — between the bad —
When God himself declines!

THE DUBS

Oh we're the Dubs, the rub-a-dub Dubs
Sometimes called 'Jackeen'
We're Prod and Papist all in one
We're Orange, White and Green!
Not King nor Pope, despair nor hope
Can make us bend the knee
From Liffeyside we draw our pride
Of Norseman pedigree.

Yes we're the Dubs, the rub-a-dub Dubs
Each mot we'll gladly coort her,
But first things first, we'll slake our thirst
With pints of thick, black porter.

We'll barrel along with many a song
And raise a glass to mine host
For life is short — let's have a snort!
And the dhivil take the hind most.

Oh we're the Dubs, the rub-a-dub Dubs
And we're a breed apart,
Don't give two shits for Gaels or Brits
No malice in our heart.
So come what may on the Judgement Day
The saints will sing our praises
No other place can boast a race
On first name terms with Jaysus!

SOLDIER OF FORTUNE

I have seen the two days, the sadness and the glory,
I have wandered strange ways, I could tell a story.
I've flattered many princes and followed many kings,
I went chasing rainbows and all such foolish things.

Soldier of fortune and everyman's fool
The billets, the barracks, my finishing school,
Hiring my courage, selling my soul,
Oh, the bullets and bayonets have taken their toll!

I have seen the two days, the fortune and the fame,
Looking for the glory instead of playing the game;
Tramping after treasure, gold and silver rings,
Blinded by the sparkle of all such foolish things.

Soldier of fortune and everyman's fool
The billets, the barracks, my finishing school,
Hiring my courage, selling my soul,
Oh, the bullets and bayonets have taken their toll!

I have seen the two days, I've soldiered and I've drilled;
I've seen the poppies growing on the fields where men were killed
As we marched behind the banners when warlike hopes had wings
And we musket-murdered brothers … and all such dreadful
things.

Soldier of fortune and everyman's fool
The billets, the barracks, my finishing school,
Hiring my courage, selling my soul,
Oh, the bullets and bayonets have taken their toll!

THE IRISH DEBATE

When our party holds its meetings
There are questions from the floor,
The agenda full of 'emotions'
And amendments by the score;
And the first thing for discussion
(Even as the Chairman sits)
Is the missing party funds
And the present party 'splits';
Then the Treasurer's Report
(Which isn't printed yet)
And the special sub-committees
(Which so far haven't met),
For the Party Constitution
Isn't too explicit
If the voting for the Chairman,
Is ultra vires, or illicit.
Oh the readin's and proceedin's
And the rulin's from the Chair
The 'objection!' from each section
And the cry of 'that's unfair!'
Oh the quotin' and emotin'
And the pompous self-inflatin'
And the grumbles and the rumbles
When the Irish are debatin'.
First a spokesman from the Left
Who seeks to clarify
Why the Party Chest — that brimming well —
Has quite suddenly gone dry:

"For them what didn't pay their subs
(And even, them what did)
Are astounded to discover
That it only holds a quid.
And the monies that were voted
For to buy new football gear
Have strangely 'vaporated
In the current fiscal year.
And likewise, Comrade Chairman,
That certain sum of cash
That somehow went and disappeared
Just before the Christmas bash?"
Oh the squintin' and the hintin'
And the subtle innuendo
And the money mention, causin' tension
And arising to crescendo,
Oh the mouthin' and the spoutin'
And the stern pontificatin'
And the sabre rattle, tittle-tattle
When the Irish are debatin'.
"I resent these accusations,"
The Treasurer now speaks,
"The mice were gnawing on that Chest
For nigh on twenty weeks,
And when I proposed the purchase
Of a mouse-trap for the shelf
The most vehement objector
Was your own cheese-parin' self!
As for that first subvention
To buy those football togs,
'Twas your own ad hoc committee
Went and blew it on the dogs!

And likewise with the Christmas fund
That somehow went amiss
It was purloined by our noble Sec
When he was on the piss!"
Oh the malice — oh so callous!
As they start into insultin'
Oh the scandals — oh the vandals!
And the ructions thus resultin'
Oh the sneerin' and the jeerin'
And the vicious imprecatin'
And the schemin' and the screamin'
When the Irish are debatin'.
Up springs the Secretary
On his face a scornful frown:
"Please suspend the Standing Orders —
I won't take, this lying down!
My honour it has been impeached
My name now bears a slur
By virtue, ipso facto,
Of that sleeveen little cur!
So, Mr Chairman, if you please
I insist we call a quorum
I'll plead my cause before the bar
Of this great and noble forum.
I am slandered and I'm vilified
And I've suffered great affront
As a consequence of placing trust
In that sneaky little cunt!"
Oh the screechin' and the speechin'
As the mounting passions throb
Oh the roarin' and implorin'
And the fury of the mob;

Oh the skulkin' and the sulkin'
And the nasty implicatin'
As they worsen — oh the cursin'!
When the Irish are debatin'.
Then the Chairman bangs his gavel
As he tries to interpose:
"Order please, I beg of you —
An adjournment I propose."
"Let us pause to say the Angelus,"
The Chaplain starts to say
And the meeting hall erupts
As the Proddies holler "Nay!"
"Order please!" the Chairman yells
"I demand that you desist!"
(But half of them with Pledge Pins
Were being thumped by them half-pissed!)
Then the Chairman struck the rostrum:
"These proceedings are a farce!"
Till a drunkard grabbed his gavel
And then shoved it up his arse!
Oh the rantin' and the ravin'
And some members in the huffs
And the hushin' and the pushin'
And the sudden fisticuffs
Oh the bumpin' and the thumpin'
And the slaggin' and the slatin'
And the kickin' and wound-lickin'
When the Irish are debatin'.
Then the Ladies sub-committee
Begin to scream and bawl
And their members, in a body,
Troop from the strife-torn hall;

"They are lacking in decorum,"
Quotes a dowager, clearly huffed;
And the chaplain, limping past her,
Mutters — "Oh get stuffed."
"Good Reverend Sir," she cries aghast,
"I can't abide these squalls."
And lifting up her ancient gamp
She jabs him in the balls.
And as he slithered to the floor
And clutched his aching scrotum
The other ladies with their gamps
All gathered round and smote 'im!
Oh gouge and grope, and 'Up the Pope'
Oh spite and bitter spleen
Oh the memory of King Billy
Oh the Orange, White and Green,
Oh the beltin' and the buttin'
And the heart a-palpitatin'
Oh the punchin' and the crunchin'
When the Irish are debatin'.
Meanwhile the hapless Chairman
Was suspended by the ears
And dangling far above the throng
from the central chandeliers;
While the half-mad Secretary
Had two tellers by the throttle
Till someone from the balcony
Hit him with an empty bottle,
And thus he dropped his cigarette
On the paper-littered floor
And the smould'ring ash soon made a flame
That crept out towards the door,

And when the place was warming up
Some member did propose
"Sending for the Fire Brigade —
Have we a seconder for 'hose'?"
Oh the firin' and the siren
And the awful conflagration
Oh the tattered and the battered
And the half-charred congregation,
Gushin' hoses, broken noses,
And the crowd evacuatin'
Oh the panic — like Titanic!
'Cause the Irish were debatin'.
Thus some of us we went to jail
And others to the Lord
And a half-a-dozen stalwart lads
To the Emer-gency Ward,
Where doctors with their surgery
Sewed up each bloody hem
So each man might be fighting fit
For next year's AGM;
Whereat we'll have the Minutes read
Of all that did transpire —
The quorums and the jorums
The fisticuffs, the fire —
And how the Ladies Sub-Committee
Are planning next year's function
And with the Chaplain's willing aid
Have laid on Extreme Unction.
Oh the sorrow on the morrow
And no more recrimination

Oh the kissin' and the huggin'
And the reconciliation,
Oh the triteness and politeness
'Midst the Party fun and frolics
… Until some lout, will up and shout
"Mr Chairman — you're a bollix!"

SING-SONG

"Sing us one of the old songs, and never mind the new,
And give us a rousing chorus and we'll sing along with you.
Oh give us a boozy ballad from the happy days of yore
And we'll raise our tankards to you, and then we'll call for more!

Sing us a song with laughter, or even one with tears
Something from the 'ould times' that sweeps away the years
Give us the songs our fathers sang, and let the rafters roar
And we'll raise our tankards to you, and then we'll call for more!

Sing us an old sea shanty, a bar of 'The Irish Rover'
Or something from the music halls like 'After the Ball Was Over'
Give us an old time favourite like 'Eileen Óg Astore'
And we'll raise our tankards to you, and then we'll call for more!

So order for the singer, silence one and all!
Whisht there, in the corner, for he has a noble call!
One voice, if you please — 'twill be closin' time ere long …
So let her rip, sagosha — only make it an old time song!"

THE OTHER FINNEGAN'S WAKE

When the last of the Finnegans died last year
To his wake a big crowd of us went,
And if all of our wages went toastin' the corpse
Then we swore it was money well spent.
Such goin's as there was comin' back on the road
As we stopped at each pub on the way
And we drank to the Finnegan boys all dead
Poor Jemmy and Timmy and Shay.

"Them three was a wojious pair," says Mick,
"A threesome if e're there was one!"
"And the father and mother of trouble," says Bid,
"And shure each was a son-of-a-gun."
"Some days you'd not see them for weeks," says Dan
"No more than you'd see them for years."
"Ah to hell with them, now that they've gone to God,"
Says Nell with a fresh flood of tears.

"Some times they were always the same," says Moll,
"And more often they tried to be not."
"Each one was a hoor for the wimmin'," says Bill,
"Yet nayther the one wed a mot."
"What lass would lie under the likes of them?"
Says Nan with an umbragey sniff;
"Poor Jemmy and Timmy and Shay," says I,
"Tonight are layin' mortally stiff."

"The more yeh say less the better," says Dick,
"'Bout them what have tragic'lly died";
"Shure their names'll live on forever," says Bob,
"And longer, indeed, if required."
"Yo'r right, yeh liar, in whatever yeh say,"
Says one of our group called MacBride,
"For the Finnegan fame went all o'er the world
and some other far places besides."

"Three daycent men, if the truth it be told,"
Said Whacker MacCarthy aloud,
"Though the gold and the silver comes to shag-all
When you're wrapped in a pocketless shroud."
"Not frequent the times when they lent me a quid,"
Said Toucher O'Brien to his mot,
"Exceedingly seldom," she wisely concurred,
"And quite recent less often than not."

"I'll never see them no more, so I will,"
With a sob and a sigh muttered Sue.
"And me too nayther, as well," says Joe,
"Shure so will I never too."

"I never was weepin' so many, no more,"
Says Liz with a woebegone grin;
"God rest 'em, the bastards," said Nosey McGurk
As he sprinkled his snuff in her gin.

And thus the porter it loosened our tongues
And thus every one had his spake
For the cemet'ry chat and the graveyard thirst
Are difficult things to slake;
So we ordered more drink, and we started to sing
To the Finnegans under the clay
And we drank the health of the glorious dead —
Poor Jemmy and Timmy and Shay.

VICTORIA-N-EDWARDIANA

— A melodramatic Tragedy concocted of evergreen favourites,
odds-and-ends, bits-and-pieces and a cast of thousands!

One night, very many years ago, I was returning from what can
only be described as a veritable Eisteddfod of recitations, poetry,
parodies, evergreen favourites, Dublin skits, Victorian, Edwardian
and Music hall ballads, etc. — in short, a real old-style Dublin
hooley! — when various well-known lines from many separate
sources (Service, Kipling, Browning, Masefield et al) kept running
through my mind.

All the way from Cabra to Donnycarney — it was nothing for
us in those days to walk to and from a good hooley! — the
colourful words continued to dog my footsteps and echo through

my thoughts, running into each other and provoking quiet giggles from Dorset Street to Griffith Avenue, so that gradually the following extravagant potpourri began to take shape.

I think it was about 4 a.m. when I quietly let myself in the front door, and although I knew I would have to be up again about 7 to cycle back to Glasnevin, and a certain printery wherein I was serving my apprenticeship, I stayed down in the kitchen transcribing my post-hooley thoughts onto various scraps of paper.

The phrases and clichéd 'one-liners' from the various originals are those appearing in roman throughout the following tale. I earnestly hope that the reader may also 'raise a giggle' as I did on that night when I discovered the charm of their juxtaposition.

It was the schooner Hesperus that sailed the wintry seas
Homeward bound from Katmandu and the heights of the Himalees,
With a cargo of yellow idols, *and a skipper called* Mad Carew
And a thousand Bengal Lancers *making up the gallant crew.*
They set a course for the Inchcape Rock *with sails set fore and square*
Crying: "Oh to be in England now that April's there!"
For the crew were tired and weary, and hadn't slept a wink
With water, water everywhere, nor any drop to drink.
'Twas Friday morn when they set sail and the ocean waves did rage
But 'stone walls do not a prison make, nor iron bars a cage'
When at last they spied a mermaid with a comb held in her hand
Says Mad Carew: "We're doomed! We never shall see land …
'Tis the curse of those green-eyed monsters that we robbed from Katmandu
They've nailed me once before, so I know a thing or two!"

Then up spoke Ralph the Rover, *his voice was soft and calm,*
"Boys," says he, "Yez don't know me and none of you care
a damn,
But East is East and West is West, and never the twain shall meet
So ye Mariners of England — *you're doomed of all the Fleet!"*
Then he lit his pipe so calmly and tossed away the match …
Which settled on the dynamite that lay beneath the hatch.
"Yes boys," says he, "this curse is true, no wonder I perspire
I'll bet my poke *within an hour this ship will be on fire."*
Now Sam Magee was from Tennessee where the cotton
blooms and grows
And he was first to see the flames that there and then arose,
"Yo-ho-ho and a bottle o' rum, and the devil has done for
the rest!"
*Sang the sprightly Sam as he sprang to the mast and raced for the
crow's nest.*

"I am monarch of all I survey!" *from up aloft he quipped*
And he did a little sailor's jig — just before he slipped!
*For the mast was tall and the mast was wet and the wind was
a whetted blade …*
Full fathoms five poor Sam lies, of his bones are coral made.

*Meanwhile, below, the flames still leaped and the gunwales
they were tinder*
The fire spread out and it quickly burned the mizzen to a cinder,
And the boys stood on the burning deck *and called out to
the shore:*
"We could not love thee half so much, loved we not
honour more!"

But Honor Moore was far away, at the burial of her dad
(Corunna town was hushed that night and the troops were
very sad)
Not a drum was heard, not a funeral note, as his corpse to the
ramparts they carried,
And poor Honor Moore, who loved Carew, was hoping to
get married!

Yet still upon the Hesperus the crew were wild with panic:
"Let's change our luck! Re-name the ship — let's christen it
Titanic!"
Sir Ralph the Rover walked the deck, he didn't fear the ashes
And he fixed his eye on a brighter speck and he saw the
hopeful flashes
"Here's the very thing we need to quell this raging fire —
An iceberg standing two miles high, a lofty snow-white spire!
Full steam ahead! Stand by the sheets … *Bo'sun be not tardy!"*
Sir Ralph then turned to Mad Carew and whispered:
"Kiss me, Hardy."
But the skipper turned his one blind eye: "Bejaysus, you're a
beauty —
Do you not know that England now, expects each to do his duty?"
Then the rush of wind, the ramp, the roar, *as the decks did*
pitch and roll
When up stepped the young lad Oliver, a-twisting of his bowl
And bravely to the captain said: "I know I am a goner …
But if you please, I would like some Moore … and I rather
fancy Honor!"

But meanwhile on a nearby shore and a-gazing out to sea
Young Mary calling cattle home across the sands of Dee
Beheld the ice, beheld the ship, beheld the awful plight
And clapped her hands with girlish glee, crying, "Oh what a
pretty sight!"
"No, no, alas!" her father cried, "help must now be sought!
I'll saddle up — bring forth the horse!" The horse was
quickly brought.
"The brigade I'll fetch," the father vowed, "the brave and bold six
hundred,
And I'll save the ship, 'pon my word, before the vessel's sundered!"
Then he sprang to the stirrup, and Joris and he
They galloped, Dierke galloped, we galloped all three
"God speed" cried the Watch, as the gate bolts undrew
And the Light Brigade followed and they raced out of view,
The hounds joined in with glorious cry, the huntsman
wound his horn,
D'ye ken John Peel at the break of day, *they'll be galloping*
hard 'till morn!
And Young Lochinvar came out of the west,
Paul Revere followed, Dick Turpin, Black Bess;
Guns to the left of them, guns to the right,
Half a league onward through the pitch black of night!
Half a league onward *through the cannon smoke's whiff …*
Till the gallant six hundred plunged over a cliff
Crying: "Ours not to reason why, *ours but to leap and fall …"*
Bill Brewer, Jan Stewar, Peter Gurney, Peter Davey,
Dan Whiddon,
Harry Hawke and Uncle Tom Cobleigh and all …
and Uncle Tom Cobleigh and all!

"Oh my, what fun!" Young Mary cried, "I hope it will not pass!"
Alas, alas, it was too late — for the ship was going fast.
Three times around went the Hesperus, three times
around went she
And all the Bengal Lancers soon perished in the sea.
The last to go was Mad Carew, a-clinging to the rudder …
"Gone, gone!" Mary cried, "and never called me Mother!"

And now when Mary milks the cows, herself and Honor Moore,
They think of all the lads that drowned, 'specially poor
Bill Brewer,
On the bonnie braes of Yarrow *they sometimes sit and brood*
And there flashes on that inward eye, that bliss of solitude,
A raging sea, the lofty ice, the flames that will not fade
A host of golden daffodils, the charge of the Light Brigade.
And down their cheeks the pearly tears often times will stray
And Mary to Miss Honor Moore is often heard to say:
"We must go down to the sea again, to the lonely sea and
the sky
And all I ask is a blazing ship — *and an iceberg two miles high!"*

THE GILFORD GUZZLERS

Goddam Those Gilford Guzzlers!
They Nabbed Me At The Bank —
Douglas, Doyle And Woodlock
And A Fellow Known As Frank —
"We're Only Goin' For One!"
They Called Out In A Chorus
Then Dragged Me To O'Reilly's
For Pints That Quickly Floored Us.

Blast Those Brunswick Boozers
So Full Of Fun And Frolics
I'm Convinced That Each Of Them
Is An Alcoholic Bollix!

Woe To The Brunswick Boozers!
I Evaded Them Last Night —
Douglas, Doyle And Woodlock
I Left Them To Their Plight;
Those Awful Gilford Guzzlers
Those Swillers Of Sandymount!
Lowering Pints Of Porter
Till Each One Of Them Lost Count;
Woe To Those Inebriates!
I'd Rather Read My Books
Than Spend Each Thursday Evening
With That Gang Of Drunken Fucks!

GOLDILOCKS AND THE THREE TEDDY BOYS
1956

"I won't sing ere a song, 'twould prob'ly take too long
And no doubt ye'd say it's all a pack o' lies,
So I'll start me little rhyme with once upon a time
There lived in Dublin town three teddy-boys.
The first was 'Gasman' Peters — he was always doin' the meters
For this was his special line in crime,
Though he could swipe a maiden's locket, or pick a bishop's pocket
While asking his reverence the time.

His oul' wan she adored him, and in vain did she implore him
To lead a life gentle, kind and meek,
And you knew he loved his mother, the way he loved no other
'Cause he only kicked her teeth in twice a week!
His other pair of mates were two gurriers off the 'strays'
And neither one could never read nor wrote
For the on'y school they knew was the toss-school near the zoo
"Heads a bob, a dollar, half a note!"

One night they robbed a fridge from a house beyond Ballsbridge
And they brung it to a place called Abbeyfield,
Though the ice-box it was hot, they flogged it to some mot
And they made a grand few quid upon the deal.
Sez 'Gasman' Pete: "That's great! Now we'll have to celebrate
So go down the flats and pass around the word,
Say 'There's free beer for all, to celebrate this haul'
And tell every bloke to bring along his bird!"
Then they hired O'Meara's Lounge, and all the neighbours tried
to scrounge
An invitation to this swell affair,
Shure half the flats were hocked in the hope of gettin' locked
And all the street was yearning to be there.

Now up round Summerhill there lived this grand ould 'thrill'
(What might be termed a gamey sort of soul)
She was fond of winin', dinin', and on her back reclinin'
And a dhivil for the jazz called 'rock-n-roll'.
She was known as Goldilocks, and she hung around the docks
Waiting for the Yankees to arrive
For it was her well-known boast that the sailors paid the most
And "All them yanks is solid at the jive!"

Now Goldilocks McCarthy had heard about the party
And as usual was rather short on cash,
So she thought she'd chance her arm, sayin' "Gatecrashin' is
no harm,
An' I mane ta say it's always worth a bash!"
The fun was in full swing when she gave the bell a ring —
(Meself it was who opened up and let her in) —
She'd a goo on for a jar, 'cause she went straight for the bar:
"I'll have a splash of orange in me gin!"

The 'do' was really toppin', there was singin' and 'be-boppin'
And the boyohs kept the gargle freely flowin',
But in the middle of the hooley they 'snaked' out for a pooley
And they left their pints of porter all alone.
When they came back from the jax they were stopped short in
their tracks
Their vicious faces quickly drained of blood
For a sight had met their gaze which left them in a daze —
Upon the bar three empty tumblers stood!
Then hate came to their eyes when it dawned upon the boys
That someone was trying to come the hound,
Up stepped Gasman Peters — "Yez lousy shower o' cheaters …
We'll marmalize the culprit when he's found!"
The second teddy-boy had murder in his eye:
"I intend to see the bastard pays the price!
Our three pints is missin' since we was outside pissin'
So what happens to our victim won't be nice!"
The third was half-insane as he clutched his 'cycle chain:
"The guilty wan had better own up,
Or we'll tear the hoor apart, from his gizzard to his heart,
The dirty ungrateful mannered pup!"

Their eyes swept round the room and they seemed to spell
out doom
As they searched around to find the guilty name,
Then they spied poor Goldilocks sitting on an orange box …
And they knew exactly where to place the blame!
Two sealed off the door, while the other crossed the floor
And poor Goldilocks sat trembling there with fright.
"So you're the little bitch that tried to work the switch,
I don't recall invitin' you tonight?
You might think you're smuckin' fart, yeh stuck up little tart,
But I've met your sort of mot around the place,
Goin' round actin' swanky, 'cause yo'r boyfriend is a Yankee
… Would ya like the stars-and-stripes across yo'r face!"

Now Goldilocks had guts and she flared back at these mutts:
"Rather have a Yank than you shower o' melts!
Just lay a hand on me an' I'll belt ya with me knee …
Try actin' Marlon Brando somewhere else!"
I pitied that poor child, 'cause that really drove them wild,
They picked her up and bounced her off the wall,
They swung her round and round, and they knocked her to
the ground
And she tore her fishnet nylons in the fall.
They grabbed her by the hair and they hit her with a chair
And two of them was kicking in her ribs …
"We'll fix her in a jiffey, she'll be floatin' down the Liffey,
And she won't go round no more tellin' fibs!"

"Oh won't somebody save me — with these bowsies do not
lave me!
They're beatin' me for things I didn't do!"

And just as she was hopin', the bloody door flew open —
In stepped a six foot bloke in navy blue!
"Oh," says she, "I'm glad, 'tis my heroic sailor lad
Straight to the rescue from New York!"
"Yerra, not a-tall," said he, "I've come up from the Lee
I've been transferred from the Gardai down in Cork."
Now the mot was in a jam, and she didn't give a damn
(You've got to act like Romans when in Rome)
Says she: "I'll see you right, if you rescue me tonight
And I'll make it worth your while to leave me home."

Now the culshy wasn't thick and he copped on there real quick,
"I don't know the hell, but she's got a gamey eye …!
These Dublin girls are flirts, but I hear they're damn good coorts
And bejabbers man 'tis always worth a try!"
He decided there and then that he'd save the little hen
And also spoil the teddies' game;
Says he: "Now clear the way, for you're going to see some play
As sure as Mick McDermott is my name!"
Then he grabbed himself a bench, and says he:
"Unhand that wench
or true as God I'll give ye all a whack!
If ye don't let go that mot then I'll belt ye in the snot
And 'clare to Christ ye'll end up on your back!"

Ah, there was really nothin' in it, it was over in a minute
He flattened our three boyohs with one swing;
And in the midst of consternation, he said,
"Now to ring the station
'Tis me duty to report this sort of thing."

Well, that's about the lot ... 'cept of course, the mot ...
We never see her now around the flats,
'Cause she married Guard McDermott, they've a house
in Ballyfermot
and they're raisin' up a gang of culshy brats.
And for their wicked life of crime the Teds are doing 'time'
Breaking stones and cleaning prison delph;
And they never did find out who drank their pints o' stout ...
Shure the guilty one was none other than meself!

PUB CRAWL

'Maid of Athens, ere we part,
Give, oh give me back my heart!
Or, since that has left my breast,
Keep it now, and take the rest!'
                                        Byron

There is a pleasant little pub in Marlborough Street, hardly a crosier's swipe from the Pro-Cathedral, called McGills. It offers its clientele one of the best pints in town and the shoulder-rubbing cameraderie of a tiny, cramped and 'snuggish' bar. Because of its lack of space (as much as its close proximity to the Pro-Cathedral) it is popularly known as the 'confession box', though the official and rather incongruous 'inn sign' hanging outside proclaims it *The Maid of Erin*.

Any pub with such a romantic-sounding title is sooner or later bound to be linked — if only in parody — with the above lines from Byron; and perhaps through those lines, with many of its sister pubs around the town.

Maid of Erin, *ere we part has the barman ere a heart?*
Give, oh give me time to state I'd like three pints upon the slate!
Or since that might seem in vain, may I call 'the same again?'
Or must I beat a quick retreat and take my custom down the street
To hie away and pocket pride, and try my luck at Flowing Tide?

Or wander to some other bar, the Abbey Mooney, *the*
Plough and Star
Or Madigan's *house, snug and cosy, and gossip there with*
Moore Street Rosie?
Or cross the bridge with eager paces — Scanlan's, Dwyer's
or then to Grace's
With docker and with stevedore to enter through The Twangman's
door?
Or Regan's *pub in Tara Street, where firemen oft are wont to meet*
(Were porter freely to cascade it could not quench our
Fire Brigade!)

Or Poolbeg Street — that famous joint, where Mulligan's *boast the*
grandest pint
And students line the ancient bar and 'Press' men down their
cutline jar —
For 'cubs' and 'comps' can quickly sink pints as black as
printer's ink!
Or Flynn's *of Fleet, and* Bowe's *nice, beside the* Pearl *of such*
great price
Where drama buffs and theatre critics quietly sip their glass
of Smith'icks
While jotting down the various scenes just enacted in the Queens
Commenting on the actors' capers for tomorrow morning's papers
With faintest praise quietly damning the histrionics and
the hamming.

Or in my quest for festive jar should I wander wide, and
forage far?
To Harry Street, and thus, McDaid, *where poet and*
playwright often paid
A visit to this fine abode to recite their latest ode.
Or Davy Byrne's, *so smart and trendy,* 'Re-may Mar-tong
and gless of shendy!'
Or other houses that I know, Do'eny Nesbitt, *Merrion Row*
Or Donoghue's *where the balladeers will sing their songs and*
sink their beers
(For Dubliners are all good sports — And there's pubs galore
up near the courts
Like Tilted Wig, *where lawyer with brief debates the law*
with petty thief,
Where bailiffs booze and 'ttornies tipple, and all engage in
legal piffle!)

Or further still — the countryside! (Ah, God be with the
bona fide!)
To step it out with marching feet to Eugene's *or*
The Sheaf of Wheat,
Or thumb a lift from passing car out to the Boot *or* Man-o'-War
Or Tolka House, *or* Cat & Cage *— where soccer talk is all*
the rage,
Or opposite end of Richmond Road The Widow Meagher's
and Gaelic Code
Or Kelly's, Cole's *or other pubs where they all booh Kerry*
and cheer the Dubs!
Or further on the road to Howth — that other inn of happy note
Harry Byrne's *of noble fame, and echoes of Bram Stoker's*
name …

But I've gone too far in 'bounds an' leps,' and must, alas,
retrace my steps
Past all the pubs of Ballybough, with visits brief, before the clock
Warns me that it's 'closing time', and puts a finish to my rhyme.

So here I am, back at the start and musing if the barman's heart
Is made of substance hard as stone — he ignores my loud
impassioned tone:
"Three pints of stout, for Goodness sake! I've a fearful thirst that's
hard to slake!"
(He's pretending that he cannot hear — perhaps he thinks I'd
too much beer?)
Perhaps he's right — I'll call a halt. "Aidan, please —
a ball o' malt!"

REMEMBERIN'

'Member the games we used to play — Nedser and you and me —
Down by the lamplit corner, and the wind comin' in from the sea?
And 'member the ring of marbles — all glassy and coloured
and bright —
And the silver sheen of the 'steeler' as it rolled out under the light?
'Member the game of 'jackstones' — the 'fingers' and the 'claw'
And then flippin' them up and over 'til your knuckles was
nearly raw?
And 'member the game of 'Rounders' and 'billy-oxtail,
one-two-three'
'Member the fun we used to have — Nedser and you and me?

And 'member the girl called Molly, and the one who was her pal?
And the freckly mot with the pigtails, and the one called
'Bright-eyed Sal'?
'Member them chalkin' their piggy-beds, and how they raised
our hopes
With their easy way of dancin' through the twirl of their
skippin' ropes?
'Member we all played 'hop-scotch', and ran to 'Relieve-ee-oh'
And they taught us 'O'Grady sez' and 'the ship in the alley-oh';
And 'member the 'ring-a-rosie' and the 'fall down one-two-three'
And 'member the time they kissed us! — Nedser and you and me?

And 'member the 'scrum'tious feasts when we queued for the
Sunday flicks?
With bullseyes ten a penny, and the black of the 'lickerish' sticks?
And 'member the toffee apples, and the paper of 'nancy-balls'?
Or the way we sucked our fizz-bags in the bliss of the fourpenny
stalls!

And 'member the 'follyin'-upper' — such terrors could
spellbind you! —
And how we tried to save the 'chap' by yellin' "Look out
behind you!"
And 'member the 'Mummy's Curse' — when we nearly done
our pee! —
For the monster kept on staring at Nedser and you and me!

And 'member the cowboy games, when our lane was a
Texas ranch?
And Nedser was always 'the marshal' and we were the tribe
of Comanch'?
And 'member our coats for goalposts as we kicked our ould
rag-ball,
And the tellin' of ghostly stories near the gate of the haunted hall?
And 'member all the sport we had when we all played
'kick-the-can'
And the hiss from the darkened doorways — "Come out and look
for yo'r man!"
And the 'blindman's buff' and the 'queenie-oh' and the homemade
Christmas tree,
And the 'tip-and-tig' when none could catch neither Nedser,
you nor me?

Ah weren't them the grand ould times, when the musketeers
were three
Down by the lamplit corner, and the wind comin' in from the sea?
When you 'member the harmless things we done and our
innercent bit o' gas
And there was no one round to tell us that them happy times
would pass.

For the pigtail mot departed — don't know what became of Moll
Though her pal became a holy nun with the Sisters of Maryknoll,
And Bright-eyed Sal is on 'the game', and poor Nedser was
drowned at sea —
And of all the 'ring-a-rosie' gang — there remains but you
and me.

STATUES

Parnell's statue starts the street, though pigeon shit doth mottle
The outstretched arm that often times may hold an empty bottle*
(No man can put a boundary mark to the marching of a nation
Much less curb the midnight drunk in the midst of his elation!)
And though we're loyal to Char-less Stewart, 'tis only fair to say
We're not so sure about respect for the 'mate of Kate O'Shea'.
And further down along the street Father Mathew turns his back
On all this vulgar revelry, on all this 'midnight crack',
Disdains the sad adulterer (and the birdshit on the ledge!)
And, silent, offers up a prayer that all might take the 'pledge'.
While still with stony, prayerful gaze he peers at Pillar grim …
And that other damned adulterer that turns his back on him
(I refer to Lord Horatio, the sailor with one arm
Who grappled once, half-Nelson style, with Lady Emma's charm)
Who now doth gaze with one good eye on the distant
Dublin slopes
While mutely memorising Lady Emma's 'Sugarloafs'.

And further on the thoroughfare, each neatly set in line,
We happen on Sir Thomas Gray and William Smith O'Brien;
The former owned the 'Freeman's' (and waterworks endowed)
The latter was a rebel who 'rabble-roused' the crowd.
Yet each in his own fashion tried to serve the nation
One with 'transpositions', and the other 'transportation'.
And next there's Dan O'Connell, the Catholic Liberator,
A noble monument in truth, a credit to creator;
There stands the uncrowned king, and at his feet there sits
A group of buxom angels, with bullet holes for tits.
Then cross the bridge and take a stroll, a noble poet to meet,
A man of many melodies — Tom Moore of Aungier Street —
(The 'Corpo' in its wisdom has aptly sited authors —
And Tommy Moore is just the man for 'The Meeting of
the Waters')
A public 'jax' he stands before, with pen poised in his mitt
As if stocktaking in his book each piddle and each shit!

And next a noble 'trinity', each renowned for knowledge
Grattan, Goldsmith, Edmund Burke, outside their native college;
The first, with hand held high, has coldly turned his back
On the one and only parliament to give itself the sack.
He faces Ned and Noll (as if round village pump)
And lambastes the dirty 'lousers' who sold out for the 'Lump':
"For they voted in the Union, in return for gold and rank!
And Henry Grattan's parliament was auctioned to a bank!"
And Noll takes note of all he says, while Neddy nods his head:
"They were mongrel-mad for money, 'tis better they were dead,"
And the 'doctor' enters in his book: "Though greed had
vanquished pride
Our land recovered of the bite — the dogs it was who died."

And thus our statues in their way have petrified the glories
Blood and tears cement the stones erected to 'ould stories';
Worldly are the effigies that excite our mild derision
('Cept for Father Mathew, he alone was of 'religion')
And each one in the thoroughfare — there's none without
a stain! —
Has engendered some affection, both the sacred and profane,
And toilers have been sometimes known their workers' cap
to doff …
And fools remain to pay respect who one time 'came to scoff'.

---

* At one time it was the custom for late-night revellers and hardchaws to
climb onto the statue and place an empty beer bottle on Parnell's hand.

INSCRIPTION ON A WEATHER-WORN,
240-YEAR-OLD TOMBSTONE

READER — WEEP NOT — BUT PRAY
WHILE TIME TO THEE IS GIVEN
YOUR TEARS WOULD ONLY WET MY CLAY
YOUR PRAYER MAY GAIN ME HEAVEN.

Friend, who speaks to us across the years,
You have our prayers, and not our tears;
We happened on your stone one sunlit day;
No doleful tears could thus damp down your clay;
Methinks your spirit mingled with our mirth —
For souls like thine must ever vanquish earth! —
And when, in truth, we join you in a while
Methinks, dear friend, we'll know thee by thy smile.

WILLIE BERMINGHAM
(Founder of ALONE charity)

Never part the 'get-rich-quick'
Or the louts with the lust for gold,
More a man of the commonfolk
With a dream for the lame and old;
Never one of the 'smart-ass' gang
Who brag that they 'have it made',
Just a straight-up bloke, who shared a joke
With his mates in the Fire Brigade.

Oh! But the places he'd been
And the hovels he'd seen —
While the rest of us cursed and raged! —
Just sparked a desire
And kindled a fire
To help the plight of the aged.

Never a man for the 'razz-ma-tazz'
Or the strutting to centre stage
More a man with a loving heart
For the captive of cell or cage
Never one of the great 'rat race'
(More often down in the sewers)
Listening, laughing, face to face
With the tramps, the pimps and the whores.

Refrain

Never part of the 'up-and-go'
More likely with 'down-and-outs'
Sharing their luke warm mugs of tea
And buying them pints of stout,
Hearing their lore of loneliness
And heeding their tale of woe,
And hoping to make their humble homes
Havens where hope might glow.

Refrain

Never part of the halo'ed gang
With candles, shrines and flowers
More a kind of brotherly bloke
Who put in the dreadful hours
Of visiting sheds with old tattered beds
And people bedraggled and liced
And where each dark stall and dampened wall
Showed the face of a weeping Christ.

Refrain

Never one of the surplice sort
Or the prelates in purple gown
More a 'how's-yo'r-father' saint
Who searched about the town
To find the old and cold and spent
And the hordes of 'Address unknown'
To help them cope and give them hope
And tell them 'You're not alone...'

ON THE LUAS

Upon a Dublin Luas Tram / Sat an old-style parish priest
Who felt it was his duty / to lecture to the least,
Beside him sat a shabby wretch / One of life's great losers
Who stank of stale tobacco / And the stench of low-class boozers,
From a pocket peeped a Baby Power / Pack of condoms from
the other
All in all, a sordid sight / to make the old priest shudder.

The wretch perused his paper: / With head intently bowed
And then moved it side to side / As he spoke his thoughts aloud:
"'Tis a qware ould world and no mistake / Of all things sent
to blight us
Does anybody know for fact / What causes the arthritis?"

The pious priest then seized his chance / and despite the whiff
drew near
"The cause of your arthritis, sir / Is very evident and clear
It's a lack of body hygiene, / Lack of alms and giving,
And all the indications / Of very selfish living!
'Tis caused by wild debaucheries / And sins beyond recall
Wicked fornications / Tobacco, alcohol!
Consorting with loose women / And here the Bible smites us!
All such sinful living / Is the cause of your arthritis!'"

The wretch remained in silence / perhaps with inward seething?
Then opened up his paper / and resumed his quiet reading.
A few moments later / The priest began relenting
Suspecting that the scruffy wretch / By now must be repenting
And with a show of some compassion / (Or in the hope it might
requite us?)
He turned to the little man: "Since when have you arthritis?"
"Ah no Father, you've got it wrong / I don't have that affliction
Even though I must admit / I have my own addiction."
"I don't have it," the poor man said: / "though I once had synovitus,
But I was just readin' here
How the Pope suffers from arthritis ..."

FAIRYTALE [OR 'WORSE-RY RHYMES']

Old Mother Hubbard went to the cupboard,
Looking for curds and whey;
But Little Miss Muffet had filled up her tuffet,
And had carted the contents away.
So Little Jack Horner was sent out to warn her,
That her action was greatly resented,
For only that day the curds and the whey,
Had swiftly and strongly fermented.
But such was his fate, that Jack was too late
— Miss Muffet had passed round the brew;
And slowly she muttered: "The gang is all scuttered ...
But I saved some moonshine for you ...!"
'Cause down came a spider, with six flagons of cider
Which copiously — hopelessly! — flowed,
And the ould Fairy Queen, brought the pints of poteen
Just to get the show on the road.
Snow White so cute, is pissed as a newt,
And Prince Charming is ever so mellow,
And Little Boy Blue is sick in the Loo
And his face is a hideous yellow ...!

And a shower of bleedin' blackbirds all began to sing
"God save the Weasel, and Pop goes the King!"
The King was in the counting house, knocking back the jar
The Queen was in the parlour, propping up the bar:
The maid was in the garden, taking off her clothes,
What she intended — shure God only knows!

Little Jack Spratt was an 'imp'erent brat,
And his wife was equally rude;
They threatened to kill poor Jack and Jill
Because of some old family feud.
So they started a row, when they grabbed the old cow
And threw him right over the moon!
And Old King Cole got a kick in the hole
When he asked them: "What are yiz doin'?"
The farmer's wife grabbed a great carving knife
And she started to scream and to shout;
But she gave a great squawk, when the big Beanstalk
Began battering her inside out!
Three blind-drunk mice were flattened twice
When they challenged the Fiddlers Three,
And even Snow White joined the fight
When she banjaxed a gnome with her knee.
And young Goldilocks kept chucking big rocks
Down on Titania's Palace,
And loudly proclaimed: "I cannot be blamed,
'Cause I'm totally lacking in malice!"

And a shower of bleedin' blackbirds all began to sing
"God save the Weasel, and Pop goes the King!"
The King was in the bedroom snoring on his back
The Queen was in the corner and was now sniffing crack
The maid was in the garden, pulling out a plum
When up came a blackbird and pecked her on the bum!

Little Red Riding Hood started to bawl,
When Humpy-Dumpy was knocked from the wall;
And all the king's horses, and all the king's men
Went back to the bar for 'the same again!'
Rapunzel, Rapunzel — how she let down her hair!
Like Lady Godiva on the old grey mare
Stripped to her pelt when she rode round the town
And she huffed and she puffed and she blew the house down.
Hansel and Gretel drank straight from a kettle
Then peed on the Babes in the Wood.
And the old wicked witch called Snow White a bitch
As they wrestled about in the mud.
The three little pigs were still taking swigs
Up till the first light of dawn,
And Little Bo-Peep started to weep
When she learned all the gargle was gone.

So Old Mother Hubbard has locked up the cupboard
And has banished the curds and the whey;
No one mentions the night, when they went on the skite
... Or the hangovers awaiting next day!

Four and twenty blackbirds all began to keen
"God save the Weasel, and Pop goes the Queen!"
The King was in the counting house, atoning for his sins
The Queen in the parlour, making Pioneer Pins,
The maid was in the garden, getting dressed behind the hedge ...
And it's 'Happy Ever After', since each one took the pledge.

THE HONKY-TONK IN OLD HONG KONG

There's a a honky-tonk in old Hong Kong, where things are
hunky-dory,
Midst the 'razzle-dazzle' razz-ma-tazz, thereby hangs a story …

That honky-tonk in old Hong Kong was run by Madam Margy
Who permitted lots of 'hanky-pank' — but never 'argy-bargy' …
And sailors from the seven seas, whose lives were topsy-turvy,
Could meet a lady for the night (once free of things like scurvy).
So 'cock-a-hoop' — from every sloop — they hurried helter-skelter
Bright and breezy, free and easy, they sought this happy shelter.

And the sailors weren't too choosey about which boosey floozie
They chose to 'boogie-woogie' 'neath the moon;
But to all those old sea-hounds, there was one girl
'out of bounds' …
A little Chinese Cracker named 'How Soon' —
Oh, such a bashful little beauty, that tiny Canton cutie …
A pearly-girly Oriental jewel!
And though secretly they sought her, she was the Madam's daughter,
And no sailor-man would dare to break the rule …

Till one night to the honky-tonk — just to try the local plonk —
Came a handsome Irish skipper named Muldoon;
And his heart went thumpy-thumpy, and he fell like Humpy Dumpy,
When first he set his eyes on Miss How Soon.
For the little Chinese bimbo had commenced to dance the Limbo —
Displaying her pretty trinkets to the throng —
And every single jingle-jangle of her many-spangled bangles
To Paddy's ears was 'Love's Old Sweet Song'.

As he chewed a curried winkle, his eyes were all a-twinkle
And they caught the answering light in How Soon's gaze;
With a teeny-weeny winking, she knew what he was thinking,
And she quietly slipped out to the garden maze.
While amidst the hurly-burly, as they played the hurdy-gurdy,
And a blinka-blonka banjo ragtime tune,
The boyoh from the Liffey, nipped out in a jiffy ...
And in the bamboo, found the bimbo 'neath the moon.

Soon 'twas smoochy-coochy, with his tiny Taiwan tootsie,
And she madly fell in love with Pat Muldoon;
For with all his ardent groping, he was hoping of eloping ...
That they'd honeymoon before the next Monsoon.
"So let's not shilly-shally, and no more dilly-dally ...
I want you as my lawful-wedded spouse!"
And with all this loving chatter, her heart went pitter-patter
Pulsating deepest passion 'neath her blouse.
Yet How Soon gently cried: "I cannot be your bride ...
Even though refusal breaks my heart!
Your plan of love, now stow it — my mother won't allow it!
And I'm afraid the two of us must part!"

And inside the honky-tonky, things went kinda wonky,
When 'twas noticed that the two had left the scene
So a baldy Burmese banker, and a lanky Yankee wanker,
Decided then and there to spill the beans.
Thus they went to Madam Marge ...
"There's an Irishman at large!
And with your daughter he has absconded!
Without your leave or pardon, he has her in the garden ...
And we all thought your daughter was beyond it!"

When she heard this awful news, her face turned many hues
And she decided on a 'show down' with How Soon
(For she had the 'heebee-jeebees', at her daughter giving 'free-bees'!)
And she swore she'd have revenge on Pat Muldoon!
Behind her was a rack (all full of bric-a-brac)
And amidst the nick-nacks was a loaded gun;
She grabbed it from its hook:
"I'll kill that Irish crook!"
So she hurried to the garden at a run.
And in the midst of consternation, Paddy offered explanation:
"I love your little daughter without doubt!"
"'Enough, your Irish guff! If my daughter's up the duff,
You must marry her before this night is out!"

In that garden sweetly fragrant, the daughter cried:
"I'm pregnant!"
Madame Marge relented without a 'Yea' or 'Nay' ...
A priest was quickly found — the two of them were bound —
(The Burmese banker gave the bride away)
And remembering to thank her, was the 'best man' Yankee Wanker,
And the bridesmaids were the floozies, need I say ...

In that honky-tonk in old Hong Kong, when things are
hunky-dory ...
The ragamuffin 'rowdy-dows' all tell the same old story,
As they strum their ukeleles — at their Chinese Irish ceidhles —
(And Madame Margy beats the ould bodhran)
They toast Old Ireland, dear Old Ireland ...
That lovely land to where her daughter's gone!

And near the motorway to Bray, there's a 'Chinese Take-Away',
And it's run by the lovely lass How Soon ...
Midst her children's happy laughter, she's living happy after
In her 'chipper' with the skipper Pat Muldoon.

POLLY AND HER PICKET

I saw her every morning
As the scabs marched down the street
In the dull and dreary half-light,
In the rain and snow and sleet.
As she clutched her tattered placard,
And held her head so high
And braved each disapproving face
That quickly passed her by.

And I cringed around the corner
While wondering at her wrong,
And slunk away in cowardice
At the echoes of her song.

Then I lingered on the streetside
And watched her bravely meet
The squadrons of the scabs,
And their heavy marching feet,
Saw her tiny, slender figure,
And eyes that never blinked
With the surety that struggles
For our liberties are linked.

So I joined her on her picket work
When I scarce knew right from wrong
And she strengthened my unsteadiness
With a smile and with a song.

And I held her hand in happiness
And I hoped that she'd be mine
As one by one, and day by day,
The others joined the line
And we stood beneath her banner,
From winter into May
Until that springtime morning
When the scabs all slunk away.

EPITAPHS

On the grave of the Dublin gurrier, on the tombstone gaunt
and grey
They've etched the words of his living, and the motto that once
held sway
They carved the words with caution, the letters strong and stark —
'What the fuck are yeh lookin' at?' was the gurrier's last remark.

On the grave of the Dublin moocher, on a tombstone smooth
and round
You can just make out his epitaph — 'Have ye e're the lend
of a pound?'
On the grave of the Dublin boozer — you can read it from afar
'Can yeh spare an hour or so, and we'll nip in for a jar?'

On the grave of the Dublin moaner, each word a well-scratched nick
'The bastards wouldn't believe me when I told them I was sick!'
And under two big granite plinths are a Dublin floozie's bones:
'For the last time I'm lying beneath someone else's stones!'

FILIGREE

'Filigree, a kind of ornamental metallic lacework of gold and silver, twisted into convoluted forms, united and partly consolidated by soldering: a delicate structure resembling this.'

Chambers Twentieth Century Dictionary

A filigree of family ties
Old friendships and the lot,
Has bound me to my native town
And wrought a tender knot;
It ties me into olden times
And lures me with its lore,
It binds me to the old-time songs
And the happy days of yore;
A lattice-work of lad and lass
Never withered nor decayed,
A soldering of ancient tales
And new ones freshly made;
A trellis of traditions
On which new flowers may grow —
To that filigree of friendships
I know how much I owe.

SONG AWAITING MUSIC

So much to talk about …
Though we've said it all before,
All the lies and alibis …
Till each one knows the score;
So much to talk about …
So many things to say …
How once we had the perfect love
And then let it slip away …
How once we had a magic dream
And we danced up in the clouds!
… But now we've drifted back to earth
And we're down here with the crowds …

So much to talk about …
Though we've said it all before,
And Love is like a garden glimpsed
Through a slowly closing door …
So much to talk about
So many things to say …
While the door is creaking inwards
And it's closing out the day …
Oh once we had the sunlit dawn
But now the twilight falls!
… And shadows creep among the flowers
And along the garden walls …

Slowly, slowly swings the door
And slowly dies the day
And silence fills the twilight hour
'Cause there's nothing more to say;
Slowly, slowly creeps the shade
Among the golden flowers
And slowly silence kills our love
Among the twilight hours ...

So much to talk about ...
But is there really any use
For another tame apology
Or another lame excuse?
So much to talk about ...
Yet we let the silence reign

For we know we've lost that perfect love
And we'll never dance again! …
A sobbing breeze from out the night
Through the garden steals once more …
And with a sad and mournful sigh
… It slowly shuts the door.

THE GREAT HAZELHATCH HORSE CRAP COMPETITION
CIRCA 1989

In the epics of equestrians / And the tales of stalwart steeds
In the sagas of good horsemanship / And the lore of Aintree deeds
In the tales of Epsom Derby / There is nothing quite to match
The great horse-crapping contest / That was held at Hazelhatch.

The punters came from far and wide / For to wager and to bet
And to view the champion crapping nag / That was sanctioned
by the vet
And they watched with great excitement / As the stewards did
then ensure
That the horse was at the starting line / And primed to
make manure.

The grass was cut, the ground was probed / For hidden snags
and snares
The field was carefully measured out / In equidistant squares,
Then each man bought a ticket / For each numbered site
Wherein he hoped the gallant nag / Would drop the winning shite.

The rules were fair and simple / And explained within a thrice:
'If the nag is in fine fettle / And he shits more than twice
Then umpires with a ruling tape / Will carefully pace the field
And with solemn perspicacity / Will scrutinize each yield;
And shall measure each circumference / And check each depth
and height
And the sum of these dimensions / Will be deemed the
winning shite.'

There were queries from some quarters / And objections from
one side:
'If the fucker only farts, sir / Will he be disqualified?'
And one demure young damsel / Was heard to sweetly mutter:
'Will extra points be granted / For a wee-wee or a scutter?'
But the stewards were firm and forthright / And they had the
final word:
'There's just one single prize / For the largest equine turd.'

The horse was hurried to the field / To one great mighty roar
As he was trotted round the course / And then circled round
once more;
And as he cantered to and fro / Across the well-mown grass
Ten thousand pairs of anxious eyes / Were focussed on his arse.

The experts viewed his every move / And tried to gauge the stop
Within the confines of a square / Where he might make his drop.
'The hoor is headin' for the hedge!' / 'No, he's swingin' to
the right …!'
'If he takes another pace or two / Square sixty gets the shite.'
'But if he circles to the left / And does another lap
Won't the low denominations / Be favoured with the crap?'

'He's boltin' round too briskly / For to make an accurate hit ...'
'If he's good at mathematics / He'll know where to lay his shit!'
'Did they feed him on the oatlets / Or a pint of jollop, was it?'
'No matter which, the big-bummed beast / Should make
a fine deposit.'

As each prognosticated / And each one tried to guess
The horse was searching for a spot / Whereon to drop his mess;
Then suddenly he halted / And slowly raised his tail —
Five thousand throats were silenced / Five thousand faces pale!
He humped his rump and bared his hole / He blasted wild
and free —
And such a heap of horse manure / I ne'er before did see!

A cheer went up, the crowd went wild / A thousand hats
were flung
And the microphone announced to all: / 'We've a champion
pile of dung!
The nag has done a noble shite / In the square marked
ninety-nine!'
As a lady cried with rapturous joy: / 'Oh, he's shat all over mine!'

She took the cup, she took the cash / The horse was led away ...
But we'll be back to Hazelhatch / And to fight another day!

A PRINTERS' ANTHEM

I have often wondered why the print industry has never produced a corpus of trade ballads analogous with, say, sailors' sea shanties, farm workers' harvesting songs, navvies' 'digging tunes' etc. Even that nineteenth-century Dublin street ballad 'Jack of All Trades' (listing more than fifty different jobs, or occupations, and the city streets where they were plied) makes no mention of printers. The nearest we get is a bookseller:

> *On Ormond Quay I sold old books — in*
> *King's Street a nailer,*
> *In Townsend Street a carpenter and in*
> *Ringsend a sailor.*

But printers have nothing bearing comparison with, or relationship to, the large body of Irish work ballads. It is a subject I once discussed with my late friend Frank Harte (1933–2005). Frank, as most readers and Dubliners know, had a life-long obsession with traditional Irish songs and had amassed a very large archive. He was a 'storyteller in song' whose knowledge and understanding of ballads was second to none. There were few singers who carried as many songs as Frank, or who sang them with such enthusiasm or enjoyment. He travelled widely, taking his encyclopaedic knowledge and his songs to France, Britain and America and turning up at almost every singers' session in Ireland. Frank sadly passed way in June 2005 having just completed another splendid album, with his friend and collaborator Donal Lunny, entitled *There's Gangs of Them Digging — Songs of the Irish Labourer*.

But to return to the subject of a lack of any 'print industry' ballads. In our pleasant discussion Frank drew a nice comparison with the old sea shanties. The shanties (sometimes spelled chanties) was the name for tunes sailors sang at work in the days of the old sailing ships. They served a very specific and useful purpose. The rhythmic 'yo-heave-ho' type of thing ensured united action in sheeting topsails, hauling ropes and weighing anchor etc. Songs such as 'Blow the Man Down' and 'I'm Bound for the Rio Grande' and the like, were sung in sets, each of which had a different cadence adapted to the work in hand. The shanties more or less disappeared from common usage when steamships replaced sail.

Could mechanisation be the answer to the print trade's dearth of melodies? Concentration on setting type from different hand-written copy, allied to what Leopold Bloom described as the 'racket' and the 'clanking', must have militated against any hopes of melody-making. 'Hell of a racket they make,' Bloom mused as he passed through the pressroom of the *Freeman's Journal* in chapter seven of *Ulysses*. The 'racket' referred to was the noise of the rotary presses in operation, along with the 'clanking' Linotype machines producing galleys of metal type. Such a cacophony could never be conducive to inspiring 'chanties'. No, we print workers really didn't have a chance. It would seem that what was required for such work ballads was the near-silent, almost monotonous repetitiveness of canal digging, rope hauling, railtrack laying, scythe-working, etc.

'Still, Capper,' Frank smiled, 'that shouldn't stop you from having a bash. You're a printer and a rhymester aren't you? Go on, give it a lash.'

Okay, and this is for you, Frank, God bless your memory.

A PRINTER'S ANTHEM

We learned to shape the letters from the writings of the monks,
From the shards of Roman pillars strewn about as
shattered chunks;
Then we moulded bits of metal for to make our alphabet
And we learned to pick the pieces so a sentence might be set;
Then we probed Old Masters' colours, and how painters learned
to think
As they pondered on their pigments — thus we made our
printers' ink.

From shreds of rags in water, we wrought each woven page
To take the first impression — and so record the age!
From dawn to dusk in 'devilment' we were daubed in inky mess
As we hauled the heavy handles that heaved the mighty press;
And gathered up the scattered sheets, and folded as we took …
And cut the page, and sewed the spine, and glued the
growing book.

Then we made the metal muscles, and the rods that rarely miss
And we manufactured Missals from the molten metal's hiss.
And made the hymns for holy folk, and printed prayer for priest,
And penny sheets of ballads for the lowly and the least;
And from the hand-made paper, that we measured out in reams
We gave the world each masterpiece — and mankind all
its dreams!

LIMERICKS

There was a young starlet called Charlotte
Who was wooed by a varlet named Jarleth
And when she was laid
He made sure she was paid
Thus the varlet made Charlotte a harlot.

There was a young artist named Jake
Who decided he'd much rather fake
He did many a Monet
And Manet for money
But never did art for art's sake.

There was a young lady so rude
Whose language I thought rather lewd
When I begged her desist
She giggled: "Get pissed —
You prissy old prick of a prude!"

STORM IN A TEACUP

You say 'tis a storm in a teacup
That it all derives from a whim,
It's all right for thee, you're not in the tea —
As you sit on the cup's golden rim.

You say 'tis a mountain from molehill
You intend not to lose any sleep
It's all right for thee, you don't have to ski
And the molehill looks dangerously steep!

You say 'tis a flash in the pan
As you poke the flames higher and higher
It's all right for you, you're not in the stew
That spills from the pan to the fire.

You say let's bury the hatchet
I couldn't agree with you more;
But you're never lax while swinging the axe
And it's my bleeding blood on the floor!

You talk about giving and taking
A concept that I'd never spurn
But you're having a ball, as I give my all
While getting feck-all in return.

So forgive and forget is the answer?
Everything else is in vain —
So I'll forgive thee, and you'll forget me —
So the whole thing starts over again!

IN MEMORY OF THE GREAT BALLAD SINGER
LIAM WELDON

They told us in the winter
That the Weldon lad was dead
Perhaps they thought the woeful news
Would fill our hearts with dread;
And though we quietly gathered round
And silent tears were shed
We knew our noble singing bird
Hadn't really fled.

There are winter times for man and bird
But they are followed by the spring,
There'll be echoes in the eventide
When we gather round to sing,
There are memories of such moments
To which our hearts must cling
Ere the tolling of a church bell
Sent our song bird on the wing.

There'll be days in darkest winter
And before the firelight's glow
When we'll belt out Barbary Allen
And join in Jinnie Joe,
When The Blue Tar Road *is shrouded*
And softly hushed with snow,
And our gallant Robin Red Breast
Will be singing soft and low.

There'll be moments in the autumn
When the morning sun will gleam
When a Lady Fair *will pass us*
And we'll conjure up a dream
As we linger on her loveliness
And bask within her beam …
Then we'll hear the love-bird cooing
And we'll remember Liam.

And as the seasons shift about
And the years go swiftly by,
We'll lilt and laugh and linger
With a song, or with a sigh,
And when ere we're sitting down to sup
Or raising glasses high
The 'Linnet of the Liberties'
Will be singing in our sky.

THE FIGHTIN' IRISH

They called us vanquished Gaels as we sadly sailed away
With O'Donnell and O'Neill, all down Lough Swilly's Bay.
The Yellow Ford was far behind — where we heaped the Saxon
dead! —
Like the failure of our Spanish friends when we marched to
Kinsale Head.
Thus we left our land to planters of the Scottish-Gaelic breed
Whom we never knew as kinsmen, for they held a different creed.

*So we sailed away with broken lords, and were left within
their lurch,*
To fight in far and foreign lands for every 'Cause' and church;
We were banished to the Lowlands, and to Rome and sunny Spain
*Where we vowed we'd ne'er be vanquished with erstwhile
Earls again.*
There we donned the divers tunics, and we plied our warlike trade
As we sought the paltry payments where the battle banners swayed.

*Then they shipped us back to Erin's Isle, when Cromwell was
the foe*
And a Roman prelate blessed us as we marched behind Owen Roe
(With a Plenary Indulgence for the sword and fire and rope —
*We could murder now for Mother Church, for Ireland and
the Pope!)*
*So they called us 'Fightin' Irish', when all we needed then
was bread*
And they lumbered us with legends all about our Fianna dead,
*While the seigneurs sought their former land and every
ancient right …*
As they galloped off behind us, after every hapless fight!
Thus they haloed us with honour, after Limerick's broken peace
As we sailed away with Sarsfield and became the ould Wild Geese.
So we served beneath the colours, for the ducats and doubloons,
*And when we died, they keened and cried, for the gallant
Clare's Dragoons.*

Hurrah! Clontarf and Yellow Ford!
Ballyneety and the Boyne!
You dub us 'Fightin' Irish'
Wher'er we hold the line!

Four hundred years have come and gone
Still history sets the trap
And on Garvaghy's country road
The spring is set to snap.

Then we marched behind Lord Dillon, and we rode with
Viscount Taff
And we massacred the Magyar, and we mauled the savage Slav,
At a time when all those peasants were uprooted from their soil
And just like us sought nothing more than bread and honest toil;
Thus we served beneath the colours for the Hapsburg and
the Hun,
And when we couldn't earn our bread we took the proferred gun.
We wintered once at Valley Forge with Washington in snow
While our clansmen and our cousins (with Cornwallis and
with Howe)
All wore the scarlet cotamore *as they fought for coins and*
bread …
And we counted half our countrymen on the fields that held
the dead.
O we served beneath the Stars-and-Stripes 'cause we hadn't
honest toil
… And we buried redcoat brothers on yonder Yankee soil.

Then we hiked behind 'Old Hookey' to the hill at Waterloo
And we showed the little Corsican a Gaelic thing or two …
Though half his troop were Irish — and we were Irish too —
We hadn't time for handshakes with the hundreds that we slew.
Oh we marched behind the banners, and we served King George
with heart!
But our bayonets broke our brothers in the ranks of Bonaparte.

Then we fought before Sebastopol, so many years ago
From there we trudged to Inkerman through wind and
winter snow
And they carried us in stretchers from the Balaclava camp
And the only one to help us was the 'Lady with the Lamp' …
Oh we murdered many Muscovites, when our ally was the Turk,
Thus we died beneath the Union Jack when they couldn't give
us work.

Oudenarde and Malplaquet!
Culloden, Fontenoy!
You call us 'Fightin' Irish'
When you need someone to die!
Five hundred years have come and gone
Still history sets the trap
And on the lands around Drumcree
The spring is set to snap.

And then the war between the States, when we donned the
grey or blue,
For the Union or Confederates we cared not whom we slew
'Our eyes had seen the glory of the coming of the Lord
As he trampled out the vintage where the grapes of wrath
are stored',
Yet we marched in time to 'Dixie' tunes, so they might not free
the slaves
… And consigned our fellow-Irishmen to most untimely graves.
We stood with Stonewall Jackson, we lumbered after Lee,
We shuffled after Sherman from Atlanta to the sea,
We rode with Grant to Gettysburg, we entered every fray —
'We toasted Ireland, dear old Ireland, Ireland boys, hurray!'

Oh, we proudly wore the Yankee blue, or donned the rebel grey
As we musket-murdered mothers' sons, when our masters
mustered pay.

Chattanooga, Antietam,
Chickamauga, Mobile Bay,
Bring on the 'Fightin' Irish'
If you hope to win the day!
Fredericksburg and Franklin
Shilo or Bulls' Run
'Give Pat another round of drinks
Then hand the fool a gun!'

Once we marched with 'Bobs' to Kandahar, and with Kitchener
to Khartoum,
Where we slaughtered many black men, and destroyed the
Mahdi's Tomb;
From there we shipped to Blomfontein with our bayonets to
the fore
And at Tugela's riverside we bashed the braggart Boer;
We trudged through darkest jungle, and we scorned the desert sun,
And we built the British Empire with the bullet and the gun.
Then back we came to dirty slums, where Larkin's word held sway
Still we turned our back on all he said and once more
marched away,
To be slaughtered down at Suvla by the Turkish shell and bomb
Or murdered by the mustard gas at Passchendaele and Somme;
Oh we fought for little nations — when our own could give
no work —
And we fell in heaps of hundreds at the hands of heathen Turk.

*Then they wrapped the green flag round us, and we fought the
Black-and-Tan
And they vowed to give us bread and toil if we rid him from
our land,
And once again we followed dreams and marched out to the fray
And they told us we were heroes if we'd join the IRA.
So we beat the Tan who used to boast 'we've murder by the throat'
Then we murdered one another for the 'Treaty' and the 'Oath';*

*For the men who made their money, and the kind who served
their king,
Could plunder all the promises when we did their killing thing;
Like the men who cite the slogans, or who sell the warlike tools
Could enlist us in our thousands when they saw such hungry fools.
Oh they knew the green and fertile land bred gobshites by the score
And we'd warlike fools and fusiliers and grenadiers galore!
So here and there the wayside cross, where Volunteer was laid,
Reminds us of the broken pledge, and still the debt unpaid.*

*So came the lure of foreign cure — the Bolshevic, the Hun —
The Fascist way, or Stalin's sway, but with each a proferred gun;
We could wrap the red flag round us, and banish every boss
We could don a brown or black shirt, and salute a crooked cross;
We could pine in fear or sorrow, or live in pride and hope,
We could march behind the banners, for 'freedom' or the Pope;
Thus the priest upon his pulpit who proclaimed a new crusade
Could pit us in our Blueshirts 'gainst the Connolly Brigade,
So back to Spain we bravely sailed to settle ancient scores
And madly stood before Madrid and Franco's fearsome Moors
While our brothers wore the red shirt and sang 'No pasarán!' …
And the olives too were bleeding when we killed our countrymen.*

Anzac Cove or Boolavogue
Valdarama or the Rhine,
They call us 'Fightin' Irish'
Where'er we hold the line.
Five hundred years have come and gone
Yet history lies in wait
And the drums along Garvaghy Road
Beat out the hymns of hate.

Still we slog behind the slogans when they cannot give us hods
Still they hail us as the heroes when we kill the Teagues or Prods,
Still we hearken to the echoes, still we hanker for the gun
Still we're marching out to murder when there's vengeance to
be done,
For we're haunted by the hatreds, and we cannot see the need
Of recognising kinsmen, though they hold a different creed;
Though we share the self-same culture, and claim to serve
the Christ
We are cursed as 'Fightin' Irish' — and we're very lowly priced! —
Five hundred years have come and gone, yet still we haven't seen
Red poppy can with shamrock grow, and Orange merge
with Green;
Five hundred years have come and gone, but there's some
don't seem to mind
That the gods that garner dead men must needs be colour-blind.

Brave men come, and brave men go
(We produce them by the score!
We've warlike fools and fusiliers
And grenadiers galore!)

But the grandkids of the noble fools
Who died upon the Somme
Did not deserve to meet their death
By a cowardly Omagh bomb!

L'ENVOI

I've boasted of my town too much,
Bombarding you with laughter and with lore;
Mayhap I've even bored you with my ploy
In trying to entertain with tales of yore.
A jester-man and porter-drinking poet
I've donned my minstrel garb of many hues,
With word and wit and whimsy for my toys
I've made a gaudy show, in efforts to amuse.
'Tis a tarradiddle town of which I'm heir —

A bustling place of boast and braggart talk
Of rowdy rhyme and bawdy ballad air
Of strum and strut and shoulder-swagger walk.
But I do love it greatly, and its ways
And with its songs I've welcomed you awhile;
So know, dear friend, the jester is repaid
If you hear his rhyme and thereby raise a smile.